What Has He Done Now?

Tales from a North West Childhood in the 60s and Early 70s

by

David Hayes

What Has He Done Now?

Tales from a North West Childhood in the 60s and Early 70s

by David Hayes

ISBN: 978-1-5272-0273-3

Cover design by Mark Shearman

Cover photo courtesy of David Hayes

Published by Bronwyn Editions in UK 2016

Preface

This book is a selection of stories from my childhood in the 60s and early 70s in a small, Northwest, mining and weaving town. This is incidental as it is about neither of those industries in particular. It is about the magic and wonderment of those days as seen through the eyes of a child – my eyes! It is about the days when imagination was the biggest plaything that we possessed. The days when a plastic football provided a whole summer's play. It is about the scrapes that I found myself in and the things that I observed around me, and how they made me feel.

All the stories are true and I personally experienced every one of them. The names of the characters have been changed. The reason being that I have no idea of the whereabouts of many of the characters contained within my stories, so I have no way of asking them for their permission to include them in this book. Some have possibly passed away, and it would be unfair of me to mention them without their blessing. Anyone who knows me will know who they are though.

This is not a novel. It is a collection of stand-alone little tales, and is in no strict chronological order. They were written as they popped into my mind. I intend this book to be like a tin of biscuits. You can dip in and consume a couple of them or sit down with a cup of tea and have a feast.

Whatever you choose I hope you enjoy.

David Hayes 2016

1960 Onwards – Infants and Junior School

I had just passed my fifth birthday when I first attended school. It was known as a 'Council School', which means it wasn't affiliated to one particular faith but was run by the local council. After the initial trauma of being dropped off by Mam (something kids these days don't experience as they have been attending nursery school for a year or two previously), I settled in and loved it. The first year of school was a wonderful time. Everything was new and exciting. We had a sandpit to play in, crayons and pencils, building blocks and of course books. Our teachers were gentle and always had a hankie ready to wipe a snotty nose or a few tears.

I already knew how to read a little before starting school, so I found it fun. Teachers would talk about word sounds and their appropriate letters by using phrases such as 'it starts with a curly ka, not a kicking ka' to differentiate between words starting with C or K. We were taught with 'Janet and John' books, from Book 1 through to God knows what number, but they worked wonderfully. Nearly all of us had good literacy skills.

Playtimes were in the school yard, which was a tarmac coated rectangle alongside the school entrance. When playtimes were over, a teacher would ring a hand bell and we had to line up outside the school door in two straight lines. Girls on the left and boys on the right. There was to be no talking and our hands had to be by our sides.

4

I remember that we had Ladybird books on just about every subject imaginable, all in colourful order in a bookcase. Some of the illustrations I can still see in my mind's eye to this day. Another thing we seemed to have boundless supplies of was Plasticene. We would play with the stuff for hours. It would start off in distinctly coloured blocks of different colours, but would slowly get mingled together until it turned into a sort of beige/brown colour. As older juniors we would model it into very realistic looking dog poo and leave it on the playground for the teachers to find. As soon as I smell the stuff these days I am reminded of junior school. Plasticene, I mean – not dog poo!

Other things I remember? Well there was free milk that came in little bottles that was like ice in winter but a bit warm and on the turn in summer. This was given out by trusted kids called 'Milk Monitors'. Each little bottle had a straw in it so that it was ready to drink, placed there by the milk monitors. I remember us having daytime naps by placing our arms on our desks and laying our heads on them. I remember having to put our hands on our heads as a punishment, but most of all I remember being instilled with a pride in ourselves and basic manners.

Our headmistress – I believe anyway – was ahead of her time. She taught us that patriotism was no bad thing, but we must also celebrate our differences. We would have what she called pageants. Children would be asked to wear their national dress to school during these pageant days. It was fabulous. There were little girls and boys in kilts of their family tartan. One boy was dressed in what I later discovered was Polish national dress. There were kids of German and Russian ancestry all wearing their clothing. Welsh, Irish, it was all there. We kids of English descent just came as we were, but in our best clothes. We would sing songs from as many of the nations that we could find, but none of them nationalistic. Songs like *Where Has My Highland Laddie Gone* and *Shamrock of*

Ireland. One Polish lad brought in his accordion and gave us a Polish folk tune. We were all most impressed. Who knew he could do that???

We were also taught that people had made sacrifices so that we had the things that we enjoyed today. Not only the brave who had fought in wars, but our grandparents and great grandparents who had campaigned for the rights and conditions of the working people. We were told that children as young as seven were working in mills and coal mines, and that poor people couldn't afford to go to school. All quite ahead of its time in many ways I think, but it made an impression on me.

Our headmistress also taught us that some families were less fortunate than ourselves and to never laugh and look down on them. My family wasn't at all rich; we were as poor as church mice, but I felt privileged in comparison to some. We had all we needed. We were fed, we were clothed, we had shoes on our feet and had an abundance of love. I often wish I could go back and tell the headmistress what a fabulous job she did, and to thank her for the gift she gave me of empathy and seeing the other person's side of things.

With a couple of exceptions (which I will go into later in this book) our teachers were a brilliant bunch. We were even taken on trips to experience other people's faiths. We went to a synagogue and several other places of worship. We were shown that all the different faiths had many things in common with our own Christian upbringing. We got to see that although different to our beliefs, they too believed in love and tolerance. I suppose, in a nutshell, we were taught to all get along – and we did!

My Den and Goodbye Scottie

Mam had a clothes horse, or 'maiden' as we called it. It was wooden and it opened out like a book. It stood some 4 to 5 feet tall and was used to dry clothes indoors in front of the fire. Nearly every house had one (we still do!). When it wasn't in service for the purpose it was intended, it had other uses. It was occasionally used as a small windbreak whilst sunning ourselves, but its other main purpose was my den.

Mam would bring down an old, woollen army blanket from the cupboard upstairs and put it over the maiden to make a small tent. I would fasten it together at the back with a couple of clothes pegs and the front was left open. With the blanket being quite heavy it allowed virtually no light through to the interior. It had a vague woollen smell about it, combined with overtones of lavender from the little bags of the stuff that Mam kept in the cupboard drawers to keep everything fresh smelling. If the flaps at the front were also closed it became pitch black inside. This is when the adventure would start. Mam would let me borrow Dad's bicycle lamp. I would pretend I was in some impenetrable jungle where tigers roamed, or exploring caves in some exotic land.

I didn't have a teddy bear, I had a little, hand-knitted, black Scottie dog, with a tartan bow around its neck. This was my trusty side-kick on all our expeditions into the darker recesses of my den and my mind's eye. Many was the adventure we embarked upon together in that little den. Our only boundaries were my imagination. Scottie was my defender and he regularly fought off the tigers and bears. I would ask him, 'What can you hear Scottie?' and in my mind I would hear him bark at some lurking menace in the darkness. No one had a team like Scottie and me; we were the best!

I loved that little toy dog. I dearly wish I still had old Scottie. Most of the kids of my generation had their toys handed on to younger kids in the family, or the neighbourhood when they were deemed to have outgrown them. I remember coming home one day and asking Mam where Scottie was, and she informed me that I was too old for it now; I was a big lad and she had given it to a family down the street. It was as if she had told me that she had given away one of my sisters or murdered my Dad. I hurriedly left the room, ran up to my bedroom and wept buckets.

I suppose Mam didn't realise that Scottie was the one I told things to and shared secrets with. He was the go-to guy when life threw up its trials and painful lessons. He listened to everything I ever said and never once told a soul. He was my little woollen brother, my one true mate. Some small part of me died that day. I never played in the den again after that. What would be the point?

The next time I saw Scottie was some weeks later. He was lying in the street with his side ripped open and all the stuffing hanging out of him. I waited until no one was looking and gently scooped him up into my arms. I gave him a kiss and said goodbye and then buried him in the woods. I think that was the first time I faced the fact that we were all mortal, and that everything comes to an end. It was also a sort of reminder that life could be brutal and unforgiving.

Now, whenever I see a little girl cuddling a teddy bear or a doll, or a little lad with his stuffed toys, I feel like having a quiet word with the parents to tell them how important these are to them. But then I just walk on by and wistfully smile to myself. I suppose they have to learn the lessons of life like I had to, and life has only one way of teaching those!

1960s – The Colours on the Lane

Anyone who hasn't tasted the humble blackberry or bramble is missing something special in my opinion. Walk down any country lane and into the fields and you would find Brambles. Horrendous strands of sheer pain that caught your clothing as you walked by them, and impaled your fingers with their vicious barbs. Entwined with these were often the beautiful, white trumpets of Field Bindweed. Add to this the hedges made of ancient, well laid old Hawthorn trees and you had a near impenetrable field boundary.

In late summer we would take a bag or a vessel of some kind and we would head off to do a spot of blackberry collecting, or blackberrying as we called it. These almost black, juicy berries looked to us like tiny bunches of grapes. These berries were our working-class grapes. They were our prize, as our Mams would bake them into flans and pies, either just as they were with a sprinkling of sugar on top, or combined with apple. We also knew a jug of fresh custard would accompany these masterpieces of culinary delight.

We would spy a particular heavily-laden patch of brambles and would jockey and jostle for position to get to the best berries. A few of the braver lads would try and push themselves into the brambles and stretch on tip-toe to reach the higher, luscious berries. The sun would usually still be warm enough for short sleeved shirts. Our arms would often look like we had been trying to juggle with cats and had come off the worst for it. Very few people seem to do this these days. If I am walking past a patch of brambles and I see a large, ripe berry, it's all that I can do to resist plucking and eating it. In fact, I often do!

The lanes were alive with bird song in those days. The skylarks ascending into the air and piping their liquid tunes until they were a mere speck in the sky. The rich, fruity tones of the blackbird and the occasional cuckoo in the distance. I knew every one of these lanes intimately and was hardly ever away from them for one reason or another. It all seemed timeless to us. It is a watercolour that resides inside my mind to this day.

After we had collected enough berries for probably several pies each, we would head off home. One particular day, a lad in our little harvesting crew told us about a trick his older brother used to do. He took out a clean, white handkerchief and put a small handful of berries into the centre of it. He then twisted the handkerchief and squeezed the resulting juice into his mouth. This was impossible to resist.

Most of us didn't carry handkerchiefs with us so we tried squeezing the berries in our hands and sucking the juice from between our fingers. All that happened was that we ended up with purple hands. One adventurous lad took off his shirt and wrapped a hefty bunch of berries into it and squeezed it and drank deeply. The juice not only ran into his mouth but all down his chest and his trousers too. 'Your Mam will kill you,' I said. He said 'Don't be daft, I'm going to wash my shirt in that pond afterwards.' This seemed like an admirable answer to the problem, so we all followed suit and were soon drinking blackberry juice through our shirts.

The impromptu little picnic over, we headed to the pond and soaked our shirts in it. Try as we might we couldn't wash out the stain, the purple was still there. The only difference now being they also stank of dirty pond water. We had no option than to wring them out and dry them on the fence for a while then head off home. We looked a picture – and not a good one in the eyes of our parents. We looked like we had been paint-balling for a week and not changed afterwards.

Mam took one look at me and could hardly believe her eyes. She insisted I tell her who had done this terrible thing to me. When I told her what had actually happened she gave me a slap round my legs and told me I was an idiot. She then asked me where the blackberries were, as she had made pastry in readiness for my return. She took my silence to mean that I had strained the lot through my shirt and there weren't any. She was correct.

Luckily we still had a bowlful of apples, so that night we had apple and blackberry pie – without the blackberries. When Mam told Dad what had happened and showed him my shirt he just shook his head and laughed. 'I would make him wear it to school,' he said to Mam. I was horrified. I would be a laughing stock! Mam said, 'No chance, I have to own the little sod.'

Mam tried everything to remove the stains. Even bleach. The green algae in the pond must have acted as some kind of mordant, making the colour permanent. I was ahead of my time. I had the first tie-dyed shirt in the street by some years. The purple-patch shirts were worn by us all for playtimes after school. Nothing went to waste. The purple stains were also our badge of pride.

The 60s – Bin Men

As a kid everyone had a traditional, zinc-coated dustbin with a lid. This was situated at the bottom of the yard. As kids we would call it a 'dussie'. Dustbins played quite an important part in our childhood. Often you would find a set of impromptu cricket wickets chalked on the side of one, or two bins would be positioned a few feet apart and used as goalposts. They were also a convenient seat, and the lid could be used as a shield when playing 'Knights of Old'.

Unlike the plastic wheelie bins of today, these truly were dustbins. The ashes from the fire would be placed inside them, sometimes whilst still hot. These made great hand warmers when playing outside on cold days. Empty bins, in November, were great to drop a banger inside, or even better a *Jumping Jack* or a *Rip Rap* as some called them. They amplified the sound a treat!

With the advent of *Dr Who* we took to climbing into the empty bins, poking a stick out from under the lid and chanting in metallic-sounding voices 'I am a Dalek, I am a Dalek'. This was much to the displeasure of our respective mothers as we would come in covered in bin dust and smelling of rotting vegetables.

The fact that one dustbin was enough for a week's waste from a family was testament to the fact that we wasted very little. Anything that would burn was disposed of on the kitchen fire. The ashes from the fire were deposited into the bin, and on it went – a small, home waste disposal unit. The only things we couldn't burn were tins and jam jars, so these went in the bin too. Most bottles were returnable, which was a jealously guarded source of income for us kids.

The bin men were a really jolly bunch which, given the heavy and arduous job they were doing, was remarkable in itself. They had a little ledge on the back of the wagon and they would stand on this and hang on as the wagon was driven from one street to the next. They would jump off the back of the wagon and pick up your bin with one handle, and with a deft swing would lift it across their backs and then tip it over their shoulder into the back of the bin wagon. I once tried to emulate this one day when the bin was about one third full. I swung the bin one handed on to my back then did a pirouette with the centrifugal force from the bin and ended up face down on the floor with the contents of the bin cascading down over my head.

One of the bin men that emptied our bins would call everyone he spoke to 'whack'. As he saw us he would greet us with 'Hello whack' and we would shout back, 'Hello Mister Bin Man'. I asked Dad the question 'Why does he talk funny, Dad?' He told me, 'He doesn't. That's how they talk in Liverpool, it's called Scouse.' It was a strange and exotic accent to us Lancastrian speaking urchins. All this made them all seem wonderful and mysterious to us. 'I want to be a bin man when I grow up, Dad,' I said to him. He just rolled his eyes and said, 'Nothing like a bit of ambition is there son?' I later found out from Mam that this was called sarcasm, and according to her was, 'the lowest form of wit'. I asked her what wit meant and she just said, 'Ask your Dad – he's been looking to find some for years.'

I did envy them, though. They got to wear big gloves and they could ride on the little platform at the back of the wagon as it drove from street to street. Oddly enough, I didn't envy them quite as much when it was pouring down or sleeting. They also seemed to lose a little of their *joie de vivre* as well and weren't quite as smiley then.

Today we have assorted colours of wheelie bins containing

13

carefully sorted (by us) individual types of rubbish. We are greener now, you see. That's why two of us now manage to fill three different bins and a box to capacity every two weeks. The idea of the happy little zinc-coated, shiny bin with its jolly tin-hatted lid now seems absurd. It wouldn't get us through until the first Wednesday.

When we go shopping we now have to buy our carrier bags, in an effort to make us remember to use our old ones, or buy a 'bag for life'. At the last count I had sixteen 'bags for life'. This should mean that I will live longer than a Giant Redwood Tree. I buy a 'bag for life' because a standard, short-lived, mortal carrier bag gives up the ghost with over two bottles of wine, and I always forget to bring them.

I have also become a 'bag for life snob'. I bought a couple of them from Sainsbury's, but transfer my shopping from Lidl into them to carry back to the car. Exactly who am I fooling? I am on Lidl car park! I also buy 'two for one' offers and usually end up eating neither, so this ends up in the bin as well. We were always told as kids, 'Eat up, there are children starving in Africa'. Just with the stuff we throw away we could probably feed two families out there.

Lately I have taken to ignoring convenience foods and buying raw ingredients. Okay, it's more effort, and the initial outlay on herbs and spices can be a bit pricey, but the results turn out way better, and the vegetable trimmings go on the muck heap. It's amazing what a few cloves of garlic and a bit of spice can do to a humble stew. The microwave thinks that I no longer love it!

To my shame, the bin containing glass bottles and jars is always healthily (or is it unhealthily?) full. Wine is made from grapes and grapes are part of my five a day. What can you do? – living healthily can be a struggle. Might as well make it fun!

1963 – Janet

They were building new properties a few hundred yards away from our ancient terraced houses. The shells of these emerging houses became a sort of unofficial playground. The damp smell of the mortar and the clean, new bricks were exciting and unfamiliar to our senses.

One day I found myself inside one of these new houses. For some reason I was on my own. I saw a girl that I knew by the name of Janet. Her parents were even poorer than mine, and as such, her clothes were probably hand-me-downs the third time over. She had a collection of old tin cans and other bits and pieces placed on the floor in front of her, along with an old plastic doll with one eye missing. She viewed my arrival with some suspicion, as she had often been the subject of cruel jibes about her clothing.

'What are you doing?' I asked her. 'Nothing!' she snapped back at me. I remarked that she must be up to something as she had all those cans and tin lids in front of her. She told me that she and Dolly were having a picnic. She looked so very sad. It touched me in some way. Other kids would have a little plastic tea set to play with. She had made her own.

'Can I join in?' I asked her. I saw her eyes checking out my face to see if this was some kind of joke. She looked around to see if anyone else was there, and maybe they would all jump out and laugh at her. When she saw I was alone, she relaxed a little and then smiled at me. I had never noticed before that she had a really kind face and a sweet

15

smile. She pretended to pour out tea for me and dolly, and finally a cup for herself.

I had never experienced the mindset of a girl before. It felt like a homely feeling. The way she acted in a motherly fashion in telling Dolly that she must wash her hands before eating. She then said, 'Or Daddy will shout at you – won't you?' Then she looked at me.

I don't know what made me say it. Call it divine intervention, but I said to her, 'No, I'm a good Daddy, I will wash her hands for her.' She pouted her bottom lip ever-so slightly and looked a little upset, and I asked her what was wrong. She shook her head and said nothing, so I asked her again. She then said to me, 'Doesn't your Daddy shout at you all the time? – mine does,' and she started to cry a little. I was useless to her. I just sat there mutely, watching her cry.

She cried for a couple of minutes then wiped her snotty nose on the sleeve of her cardigan and turned to smile at me. She then gave me a hug and said 'You are nice. Can we be friends?' I told her that we already were. She told me all kinds of things about her home life. It sounded a little grim. Apparently it was her stepfather. I didn't ask what had happened to her real Dad, I just assumed that she would tell me if she wanted to.

I told her that it was my dinner time and Mam would be shouting me in soon. I asked her if she wanted to come home with me, and that Mam wouldn't mind. I told her I was always bringing friends back unexpectedly. She shook her head and looked very nervous about the whole idea. 'Aww go on, she's nice,' I said. She reluctantly agreed.

I arrived back home and asked Mam if Janet could have some dinner with us. I found out later that Mam knew all about the family and how the wife and Janet were the victims of his bullying. Mam looked at her pathetic little form and said, 'Of course she can. Come on in, love.' She then asked her if she liked eggs. Janet nodded eagerly and said 'Where do I wash my hands?' Mam remarked that she was a good little girl for not needing to be asked to wash her hands, and could she teach me some manners too. She giggled.

Janet ate her eggs and toast with a look of sheer bliss on her face. We never usually had any afters during the week at holiday dinner times. This was usually kept for after our tea in the evening. Mam announced that seeing as we had a guest she would open a tin of peaches and evaporated milk. I had figured out why, and just pretended this was normal. The last thing I wanted her to feel was awkward, or as if she was some kind of charity case. Janet began to relax and was quite a talkative little thing. Mam smiled at her and told her that she was such a clever girl.

When dinner was over she asked Mam if she could help with the washing up. Mam said that it was fine and to go out and play, but she said 'I'd like to... can I help?' Mam's face broke into a soft smile and said. 'Of course you can, love'. There they were, chattering away together. Janet standing on a stool to reach the sink and wash the pots and Mam drying them with a tea towel.

We became good friends, even though my mates made fun of me for liking a girl. I didn't care. I liked Janet. Eventually our houses were pulled down too and we went to different areas of town and we lost touch. I later heard that she had done well at school and studied hard and was now a senior nurse. It didn't surprise me in the least. I never forgot that little picnic we had with tin cans inside the shell of that partially built house. I think the owners might be tickled pink to know it.

17

1963 – Miss Angel

At junior school we occasionally played host to the odd student teacher. Usually they were there to be tried out with some actual teaching experience. They came and they went without barely registering on the scale, with one memorable exception in my case. Her name was Miss Angel.

It was during class one morning. We were being taught by Mrs Evans. A lovely 'old-school' type of teacher (no pun intended) who insisted we behave but was a gentle, sweet old soul. In walked the headmistress and announced, 'This is Miss Angel, please say hello class.'

We all answered in unison, 'Hello Miss Angel.' Standing before us was a breath of fresh air.

She couldn't have been any older than about twenty but, unlike most of our other teachers, she had really modern and refined dress sense. She also wore a small amount of make-up, and a delicate shade of pink lipstick – unheard of with the traditional lot at our northern outpost. Mrs Evans gave up her post and, with a smile and a touch of Miss Angel's shoulder, she announced, 'I'll leave these little terrors with you,' and with a gentle chuckle, she left the classroom.

Miss Angel said hello to us in a silky, beautiful, refined voice and asked us if we would like to ask her any questions. This floored us for a moment, but soon the questions came thick and fast. It was the girls who led with the first foray of probing questions, such as, 'Are you married, Miss?' and 'Where did you get that skirt, Miss, it's lovely.'

She informed us that she was single and bought her clothes in an exotic and wondrous land that we had never heard of. It was apparently called Knutsford (in actuality only about twenty miles away – but it is in rural Cheshire. It may as well have been Mars to us).

She soon had us involved in all kinds of activities from drawing to counting games. She drifted like a vision from desk to desk, doling out praise and small hugs in equal measure. She approached me and asked me my name. In embarrassment I looked down at the floor and mumbled, 'It's David, Miss.' She then placed her beautifully manicured finger beneath my chin and lifted my head to look at her. She said, 'Am I that ugly you can't look at me? – oh dear, I hope not.' Then she laughed.

I just blurted out, 'No Miss, I think you are beautiful.'

She beamed a perfect white smile at me and said, 'I think you are too, you have lovely blue eyes, don't hide them away.' Then she gave me a hug and moved on.

I don't think anyone had ever paid me a compliment. Certainly not a teacher, apart from the occasional 'good lad'. I didn't quite know how to react. I only know that I instantly fell in love with her there and then. Not in any sexual way – good God, no. Girls and kissing were repulsive to us at that age. I fell in love as would someone who had seen the most gentle and beautiful thing and wondered if they were dreaming and about to wake up. She was radiant, confident and assured.

In one lesson we were all in a circle on the floor and Miss was sitting on a chair talking to us about colours and how nature used them for camouflage and defence. She then asked us what our favourite colours were. Most of the boys came out with macho answers such as 'I like black Miss' and she would smile at them

19

sweetly. When it came to me I answered, 'It's blue, Miss.'

She said, 'That's my favourite colour too,' and then she wrinkled her nose at me and gave me a little smile – it made my day!

She never criticised us for our working-class, northern accents. But she would occasionally say things like, 'Try and say it's really good and not it's proper good.' Then she would smile and ruffle someone's hair.

To a person, every kid in that class adored her. The girls saw her as the big sister they wished they had and the boys were just disarmed by her gentle, fun ways.

All too soon her brief stay was over. It would be about a month in total. The headmistress announced that Miss Angel's time was up with us and that this was her very first teaching post and we were all to show our appreciation. We clapped like mad people. The headmistress said that she would leave Miss Angel with us so that we could say our goodbyes.

I don't know when it started but a few girls started sniffling. Soon most of the class was in tears. We were asking her questions like, 'Do you have to go, Miss?' and 'Don't you want to stay here? – we all like you.' She could hardly answer us. Her voice broke a little and she said, 'Oh please children, don't cry. I just can't bear it.'

We had what the Americans would call a group hug and all too soon she was leaving. As she brushed past me she turned her head and said to me, 'Always keep that pretty head of yours up, David.' Up until then I had been able to hold it together. I just dissolved into tears. I saw her glide off through the door through bleary, tear-filled eyes and she was gone. The class was in grief.

It was good old Mrs Evans who rode to the rescue with her gentle but brisk 'Come on children, this will never do. Let's all be brave soldiers.' She told us all to put our arms on the desk and place our heads upon them as a nap was the best thing to cure tears. For minutes after you could still hear the odd sniff and sniffle. When we awoke it was as if it had all been a beautiful dream.

I genuinely wish I could tell that delightful lady (because she was indeed a lady in the truest sense) how much she opened these 'pretty blue eyes' of mine. She gave me a glimpse of a gentler and more refined world. She gave me something to aspire to that was above the mines or the mills. I raise a glass to Miss Angel, the most aptly named person I ever met.

Mam's Cooking – 60s Dinners.

My mother cooked all our food for us as did all mothers in those days! When Mam cooked something, it got cooked – thoroughly. We didn't have steamed vegetables that were crisp and al dente, and still shiny as if fresh from the field. No, these were boiled until they were as saggy as elbow skin. Spuds were either fried as chips or peeled and boiled to the point where they just about stayed together.

It was the same if we pushed the boat out and bought a joint of beef for Sunday dinner. It would be cooked until it was about two thirds its original size and a uniform brown throughout. We never had the tender, moist, pink centre like they did on Masterchef. This to Mam would be considered raw. All this said, I adored it. Gravy was made using the juices from the meat, gravy browning and a bit of cornflour to thicken it. In the middle of the table would be rounds and rounds of buttered bread on an old Willow Pattern plate.

Her Yorkshire Puddings were a thing of joy. Soft and fluffy as kittens inside but golden and crispy on the outside. When she cooked pork chops the fat would be crispy on the outside, but when bitten into the centre was soft and luscious – the juice would run down your chin in a glorious, full-flavoured, greasy torrent – nectar!

It wasn't Nouvelle cuisine either with the vegetables arranged in an artistic pattern on the plate with swishes of different coloured sauces adorning the creation with a small medallion of meat setting off the picture. This stuff arrived on a big ladle and came in industrial proportions, served not with a cheery 'bon appetit' but a

'Get it eaten, there's nothing else 'til tea time' – and eat it we did!

When we asked, 'Is there anything for pudding Mam?' We would still be eating our meal. She would answer, 'Yes if you eat up', then she would produce something like a lovely, home-made rice pudding. I loved the brown skin that sat on top of it. The best bit in my eyes. I would either sprinkle a bit of sugar on top of my rice pudding or would ask Mam to bring out the jam so I could stir a spoonful into it. She also made a lovely Lemon Meringue, a family favourite. Not the crispy meringue but the one with soft, fluffy peaks on it that melted in your mouth.

She learned her cooking from my Gran (or Nanna as we called her). No doubt she was taught by her mother too. Nothing was processed (unless it came in a tin like peas or beans), no Monosodium Glutamate or E numbers. Just whatever was in season and on the horse-drawn fruit and veg cart that toured the streets, or at the corner shop or the butchers. We thrived on it. We would fill our bellies then run outside and work it all off by playing footie in the street with games that could last three hours at a stretch, or playing tick or hide and seek. We were rarely still. Come tea-time we were hungry again. Then came the familiar cry of, 'What's for tea Mam?' which came with the answer 'Nothing until you wash your hands, and wipe your feet, I've just mopped in here.'

Although we had a hot meal inside us and it was plentiful, it was what you would call, 'no frills plain cooking'. The monotony of the boiled spuds was off-set by our hunger and the knowledge that this is all there was. No opening the fridge for a yogurt or to the cupboards for a packet of crisps or some chocolate biscuits. There weren't any. Come to that, there wasn't a fridge either!

I remember the arrival of fish fingers on the food scene. Although a staple of kids' food these days, in those days it was considered by us to be a luxury item! With not having a fridge or a freezer they had to be consumed that day. Occasionally we were treated to a tin of

Spaghetti Hoops or Alphabetti Spaghetti. We would try and spell out rude words on the side of the dish and giggle whilst we did it, then quickly eat them before Mam noticed.

Friday was always 'chippy tea' and Sunday was always a proper Sunday dinner of meat and two to three veg. The only convenience food was the chippy, dried peas that were steeped overnight to make pea soup and tinned stuff. Sometimes the Ice Cream man would come around, and if any money was available we would get a treat. Apart from that there was nothing else – unless you were rich, and I didn't know anyone who was!

We got our spending money for the week – mine was two shillings. So if we wanted comics, sweets, a packet of crisps or a bag of chips in the evening, it all came out of that two bob!

For a little while I got a job at a wood yard, chopping and bundling up firewood for the owner to take around the shops and sell. I worked a couple of hours a night Monday to Friday and earned the princely sum of half a crown. With my first week's wages I went in to town and bought Mam a huge block of Cadbury's Dairy Milk. When I gave it to her she said to me, 'Oh love, you shouldn't go spending your money on me – you worked for that' I just said to her, 'Well I know you like chocolate.' She gave me a hug and thanked me. I could see tears in her eyes. I suppose I bought it in the knowledge that it would be shared out amongst us all equally – that's what we did! I just liked the idea of feeling like the man of the house and a provider for a while!

When the Canal Still Carried Coal. Mid 1960s

When I was around the age of twelve or so, a couple of friends and I would take a walk down to the canal and wait by the swing bridge for the narrowboats to come through – or barges as we called them. They would carry coal from the pit to their destination. In this case it was Wigan.

As the barges approached the swing bridge, we would shout to the driver (or whatever they call someone who steers a narrowboat), 'Hey mister, give us a ride!' Some would just bark 'NO' at us, some would use more colourful language, but occasionally one would say 'OK, jump aboard.' We didn't ever need asking twice! One particular bargee was a nice old chap. Always had a smile on his face and whistled through his teeth as he went about his job. He was one of our favourites.

One particular day he told us that he fancied a cup of tea as he hadn't had a brew for hours. He pointed at me and said 'If I give you the tiller, do you think you can steer in a straight line?' It was as if someone had handed me the keys to Concorde. 'Yes I think so – yes, yes I can,' I answered. He said 'OK, put your arm over this tiller and keep it in a straight line. If it starts drifting to the right then move the tiller to the right and it will move left. Got it?' I said that I understood. He then told me that if I saw a boat coming the other way to gently ease the tiller to the left a little and shout loudly for him. I fully understood what he meant and would have shouted like a banshee if I spotted anything within a mile. He went down into his cabin and was whistling merrily as he watched his kettle boiling on the stove.

It was wonderful. The gentle 'thud thud' of the diesel engine, the smell of the warm oil and the smoke from his stove. We gently cruised along and watched the world pass us by at a gentle pace. The boat just seemed to hiss as it cut through the water. Swallows and Sand Martins wheeled and dived in front of us, catching insects almost effortlessly as they chattered and screamed. A happy little Mallard guided her offspring past us. She and her ducklings riding our bow-wave like a roller-coaster. We felt as if we were part of the scenery – part of nature itself. It just didn't get any better than this!

Some minutes later, and refreshed after his cuppa, he smiled at me and said 'Well done bosun – I'll take the helm now,' and he saluted me. I gave him a rueful grin and handed back control of his boat. I thanked him very much and told him it had been 'magic'.

We did earn our keep though. Between us and our destination there were twenty-three locks to get through. After showing us how everything worked, we helped him with the work of opening and closing the lock gates. We didn't mind in the least!

When we finally reached our destination, we would have a walk around Wigan town centre before making our way to the bus station. There we would each buy a carton of strawberry milk out of a vending machine on the platform and catch the bus home.

That night I hardly got any sleep. In my dreams I was still piloting that barge!

1960s Bonfire Night

"Remember, remember the fifth of November, gunpowder, treason and plot".

This was a rhyme that every schoolchild in Britain knew, as every fifth of November huge bonfires were (and still are) lit and fireworks let off. It was to commemorate the capture of Guy Fawkes in 1605. He had placed several barrels of gunpowder under The Houses of Parliament and was going to blow up the government.

For maybe a month prior to this date, kids would gang together and each street would gather wood for their bonfire (or Bommie as we called them). This wood was guarded jealously as "bommie raids" were quite common. We did a few ourselves. Inside these stacks of wood we would build little camps. Somewhere to sit on dark evenings and tell eerie tales or smoke illicit cigarettes. I remember one year we had started particularly early and had amassed a huge pile of wood. One or two of the neighbours began to get worried that this was getting out of hand. Strange to relate, a week or so later, this mysteriously caught fire late one night – fancy that, eh?

More importantly, even as children, we were allowed to buy fireworks. These were saved in an old biscuit tin for the big day (but many weren't). The temptation was far too great, especially with threepenny bangers, a type of firecracker with a ten second fuse (just long enough to beat a hasty retreat) rockets, jack-jumpers and, best of all, Air Bombs. These shot projectiles like a Roman Candle that then exploded with an ear-shattering noise. We would fasten these with string to a piece of wood and use them like a sort of gun. We would get up to all kinds of firework related mischief.

I remember going to the shop with a bunch of friends and buying a particularly large rocket. I had saved up to buy it. On the way home I tripped and stumbled against a wall and the stick broke off about three inches from the body of the rocket, so we decided to pick a quiet moment and set it off that night. No one knew what the reason for the stick was anyway – we thought it was just so you could slip it into the neck of a bottle to let it off – we were soon to find out!

We put the remaining stub of the stick into the neck of a coke bottle we had rammed into soft earth and lit the fuse. The rocket ignited and veered off sideways like a wayward Exocet missile – bouncing off house walls and almost taking my head off. So that's what the stick was for – stability!

Eventually (as designed), it exploded into a myriad of crackling, spitting little mini explosions. Unfortunately, it did this three feet above a neighbour's greenhouse. We were stunned as it basically took the roof off in a shower of glass. We looked at each other for what felt like a lifetime, until we saw his porch light come on and we beat a hasty retreat.

We were also allowed (basically, in a nutshell) to beg on street corners. Children made a sort of effigy of Guy Fawkes out of old trousers and jumpers to be burned on top of the bonfire on the glorious 5th. Prior to this, we would sit it on street corners and yell at passers-by "Penny for the Guy?"

We grew quite adept at Guy making and begging. All money raised was shared out equally and spent on fireworks for the big day. One year, for whatever reason, we didn't make a Guy (a horrendous oversight!) – how were we to extort money out of passers-by? We came up with a cunning plan. We dressed up Neil, the youngest of our little gang, in old clothes and a balaclava and face mask and sat him on the pavement as our Guy. Two burly miners were walking home after a shift down the mines. "Penny for the Guy misters?" we entreated.

"That's not a Guy that's a kid dressed up," one of them said. We assured him it wasn't. "Okay then, I'll give you half a crown (12 and a half pence, a king's ransom back then) if you will let me kick it." Neil gave a sort of panicked and muffled "NO" but we silenced him. "OK mister." I had made the deal! – He handed over the money. He took a run up like some fast bowler in an ashes test, and a split second before impact, Neil let out a frightened scream and got up and ran like the devil himself was after him.

We all ran off and peeped from behind the corner, but instead of seeing what we had expected to see – two angry miners – we looked back to see them both convulsed in laughter. I distinctly heard one of them say, "They were going to sacrifice that poor little sod to a broken leg for half a crown." – and we were!

1963 Knock, Knock, Who's There?

Anyone who has played 'Knock and Run' will not need the details of this particular piece of mischief explaining, but for those of you who haven't, the rules are fiendishly simple. You knock on someone's door and run away – preferably very quickly! The adjoining street to ours was perfect for this, as the front doors of the terraced houses opened out directly onto the street. This meant no awkward paths and gates to negotiate our way out.

All the neighbours knew who it was, or had a pretty fair idea, but if they didn't see us then they couldn't 'dob us in' to our parents. We would know if they had because the cry of, "I've seen you. I know who you are, you little buggers!" would ring out after our retreating steps. Then we knew we would be in for it. We played this game at least once a week.

The game started to feel a bit stale. You knocked on someone's door and ran away. Big deal! So we started thinking up ways of spicing it up a little. One game we played was to gently prop a piece of wood against someone's door at such an angle that it would fall inwards into their hall when they opened the door. This in itself was enough call for hilarity as it would scare the living daylights out of them as it fell in.

This also began to get ramped up a little as we sought bigger thrills. The final incantation of the game was to prop the piece of wood against the door as before, but this time balance a sterilised milk bottle on top of it full of water so that it would definitely smash.

Glass AND water – what could be better? Finally, to add insult to possible injury, the last liquid we used was our own urine. We were severely reprimanded for these acts by our parents so we behaved ourselves – for a while!

I think it was me who had the idea of tying all the door knockers along the row together with a length of kite string, and with a boy at each end, the string would be violently jerked outwards, thus activating all the door knockers together. It didn't work that well as the middle ones didn't move at all, but the first three houses at each end almost had their door knockers torn off. Back to the drawing board.

An older boy told us a ruse that his Dad had told him that they used to do as kids. Probably not an advisable thing for his Dad to do. Did he think we weren't going to try it? We scoured the streets and collected dog poo in an old can. We must have collected a good pound in weight of the stuff. This was then deposited on to the doorstep of the victim. On top of this we put a few pieces of crumpled up newspaper, we then set light to it, knocked on the door and ran to hide. He came out to see who was there and was confronted by a small fire. He did what anyone else would do. He stamped it out with his foot – his BARE foot. We heard him exclaim to the occupants of the house 'Oh God, bring a cloth; they made me stamp in dog shit'

We then invented a game called 'Mam says'. This involved knocking on a neighbour's door and saying, 'Mam says can she borrow a cup of sugar?' or some such thing. We would then take it back after about fifteen minutes totally untouched, and say something stupid like 'Mam got it wrong, she meant raisins. Have you got any raisins?' If they had, we would repeat the exercise over again. The excitement was knowing when to stop before getting caught and getting a clip round the ear. We once got three steps along from sugar and stopped short of asking for a tin of peas, as even we thought it too ridiculous.

This particular series of games was brought to a spectacular halt by a plot that all the neighbours had hatched together with our particular Mam's and Dad's. We were all summoned to appear at the house of one of our gang. As we walked in we saw six or seven of the neighbours there, but more alarming was the sight of the local bobby. One neighbour spoke up and pointed at me and another boy and said, 'Those are the two. They stole a cup of raisins off me.' What stopped me from instantly filling my pants, I have no idea.

The policeman then said that theft was a very serious offence, and we were all present at the scene of the crime, so we were all equally guilty. He then mentioned that the judge may take pity on us as this was our first offence and that we only might get a light sentence. Probably only a year in Borstal!! So there I was, a nine-year-old staring down the barrel of a prison sentence. I don't know who burst into tears first. It was a pretty close run thing.

Suddenly we were offered a lifeline. The policeman asked the neighbour whether he wanted to press charges. We looked at him wide-eyed with pleading faces. He then said, 'Yes, throw the book at the little buggers.' At that, all the adults in the room burst into guffaws of laughter, the policeman included. After a short while, and when we had stopped crying and our bowels had returned to normal, the policeman sat us down and gave us all a lecture about being good lads, and that we were now all on police record (a lie, but we believed it). For at least a month after that we made Mother Teresa look like a Hell's Angel. We were exemplary... but all good things come to an end!

1964 – Junior School

I have a love of the written word and literature in all of its forms, from great poetry and the classics through to contemporary, modern writings. The term 'Get lost inside a book' to me is just that. I allow the narrative to take me by the hand and lead me into another strange and unfamiliar world.

I believe I owe this to one particular teacher at junior school. Not only would he try and make all lessons interesting by often turning them into a game or a competition, he would read aloud to the class. These times were pure magic. Not one child messed around or became distracted. He held us all in thrall. He read us such classics as *Three Men in a Boat* by Jerome K Jerome, but the one book that had the biggest impact on us all was *The Lion, The Witch and The Wardrobe* by C.S.Lewis.

This book had the class totally mesmerized as we were led, by his words, into the magical land of Narnia. He wouldn't merely read the words out loud, he would almost act them by giving certain passages dramatic gravitas. I remember when he came to the part where Aslan died. Many in the class were openly weeping. He would read so far into a book, for possibly half an hour or so, then stop just as something exciting was about to happen. He was the first to adopt the Eastenders type ending, but instead of the drum solo he would merely say, 'and we will have to wait until tomorrow to find out what happens'. A chorus of 'Awww no sir, tell us what happens,' would immediately ensue and he would merely smile and carefully close the book and put it away.

He would also encourage creative writing. He once set us an exercise to write a short essay on a favourite painting we had seen and we weren't allowed to use the word 'like', thus forcing us into being more creative. He said, 'Use the words resembled, or compared to, or see if you can all think up different words that mean the same thing.' He taught us what similes were and said we could use those – white as snow, tight as a drum – 'those kind of things,' he said. It forced us into being more creative and painting with words instead of merely making statements of fact. We had a good scattering of these wonderful teachers. These people made coming to school a pleasure – but some didn't though!

One teacher in question took an instant dislike to me and another lad in my class. The harder we tried the more he would pick on us. One day he was firing out questions on the times tables to the class. He would point at someone and say things like, 'Sylvia what is three times four?' or 'John what is six times two?' He then pointed at me and said 'David, what is nine times seven?' I had to mentally run through the sequence in my head, but he never gave me time. 'Stand on your chair boy and tell the class that you are stupid.' So I did as I was told. He left me standing on my chair for about twenty-five minutes until the lesson ended. I was a shy boy and he knew it. This was ritualistic, public ridicule.

One of my friends told Mam what had happened and she asked me, 'How long has this been going on for, love – him picking on you?' When I told her around six months I saw her lips tighten. The next day she walked me to school a lot earlier than normal. We walked to my form classroom and he was there with his cup of tea and his pipe in his mouth. When he saw my mother – all five feet two of her, he looked startled. Mam strode up to him and said, 'When my lad is naughty you have my permission to give him a smack or shout at him. YOU DO NOT have my permission to break his spirit or humiliate him – DO I MAKE MYSELF CLEAR?' He merely nodded. She then lashed out like a cobra and knocked his pipe right out of his mouth in one deft swipe, sending it clattering across the floor and under the desks. She then stood almost nose to nose to him and proclaimed, 'When my son grows up, he won't have to smoke a pipe to make him look like a man. You are nothing but a bully.' Then she strode to the door and turned to face him again and said 'remember – I will be back if you don't.'

He was as different as night is from day after that, with me, and the other lad come to that – especially when he asked what our parents did for a living and the other lad answered, 'My Dad carries bricks in a hod up ladders sir' – I think he didn't want a burly, big brickie paying him a visit either!

1960s – Airfixation

As did most big towns of the day, we had a toy shop. It sold everything from teddy bears and dolls to train sets and dinky toys. It also had an extensive range of Airfix models. I think it was the exciting graphics on the box of said aircraft, vehicle or ship in its natural surroundings that we fell in love with. The contents often disappointed us. We would walk into town clutching our spending money and head towards the toy shop in eager anticipation.

We would stand transfixed in front of the dazzling array of boxes as we trawled through all the names and types of aircraft they had in stock (aircraft were our particular speciality. Who the hell wants to play with a galleon?). We would try and get our northern tongues around such names as Messerschmidt ME 109, and the far more risky to pronounce Focke Wulf FW 190.

I think most boys started off with the same choice for their first attempt at an Airfix kit – The Spitfire. When we bought our first Spitfire models, we quickly realised that if we wanted it to look remotely like the picture on the box, we needed to buy several colours of paint. It was startling when you realised how many colours you needed to make a faithful representation of a Spitfire in all its colours. You needed the two colours for the camouflage. Black for the tyres. Silver for the wheel centres, and if you wanted to paint the little pilot you needed even more – on and on it went, so we didn't bother.

If glued together correctly, the propeller could be turned, and also the wheels would turn. You also had to be very sparing with the little tube of glue that they gave you with the kit. We just glued everything together in our haste to get it finished and play with it. So what if the propeller didn't turn! The little roundels on the plane's wings and body were also somewhat unnecessary to us, and why did they insist on calling them decals? I stuck mine on each side of the front mudguard of my bike.

As our skill levels (and patience) increased over time, we started making and painting them properly. I had amassed dozens of little tins of Humbrol paint and kept them on a little shelf in my bedroom with the labels to the front so I could select the correct colour with ease. Yes, I was a sad little nerd, but then again, so were my mates. They were all at it too.

Once you had assembled your aircraft you then had to fasten bits of fishing line on them in just the right point of balance, and hang them from your bedroom ceiling. I had my Spitfire (now far better assembled) hanging just behind the Messerschmidt ME 109 as if it were chasing it in a dogfight and about to close in for the kill.

My Lancaster Bomber was suspended in a perfectly level manner by two bits of fishing line in front of my bedroom window. At night, when the lights were off, I would draw back my bedroom curtains and the bomber would be silhouetted against the night sky outside. I had a little torch that I would shine in slow circles around it. I imagined this to be a German spotlight and pretended it was on some treacherous bomber mission deep behind enemy lines. Actually it was very convincing when viewed as a silhouette against the window. If you took a photograph it would actually look like a 'Lanc' flying past the window.

Once a model had been made, it had to pass the 'Mates' test. We were critical of each other's skills, and we would say things like 'You ran over with the paint a bit there' or 'That decal (yes, we were now

37

calling them decals too) is a bit closer to the body on that wing than the other'. I once remember our little gang knocking on a neighbour's door to settle an argument over whether some lettering was level or slightly off. He just told us to 'sod off'. Fair comment really as Morecambe and Wise were on the telly!

We branched out after a while and started assembling sports cars and ships, but our first love were the flying machines of 1939 to 1945. The habit got really bad with us. We were constantly begging our parents for money for our 'Airfix fix'. I think we must have been high on the glue! I once remember asking Dad if I could borrow four bob. He said, 'Well first of all, no. You still haven't paid me back the two bob I gave you last week, and secondly, what do you want it for?' I said that I had set my heart on a model of a Short Sunderland at the toy shop. He said to me 'Well you are halfway there, you *are* a short ARSE, that will have to do.' I gave him a sickly, sarcastic smile and said 'Ha, Ha Dad, you are SOOOO funny.' To which he answered, 'Yes, and rich. I have four bob and you don't.'

Some years later, and long after we had stopped making the Airfix models, we put bangers under or inside them and blew them up. It was our idea of special effects, like in the films on telly. Sacrilege really. I wouldn't dream of doing it today – but then again I am a big kid again – and yes, it I had a model 'Lanc' I would still hang it in front of my bedroom window with bits of fishing line. I don't think I would play at searchlights though!

Early 60s – Fighting

If you went to school in the 60s, you would inevitably end up in a fight. At junior school (from about the age of six) I had to wear glasses. These were what were called 'Clinic Specs' or glasses provided by the NHS. These were little round-lensed efforts not unlike the Harry Potter style glasses, but they had a sort of half-round sprung clip that fastened behind your ears. This gave the glasses remarkable stability. I doubt they would have come flying off in a plane crash!

Not only did this bring the inevitable taunts of 'Specky four eyes', but also, with the advent of *The Milky Bar Kid*, a new and consumerist taunt of 'Hey Milky Bar'. One day I had been subject to quite a few taunts and jibes referring to my facial attire, and I just lost it. I snatched the offending glasses from my face, and whilst issuing forth a maniacal, animalistic scream, I crumpled and twisted the glasses into a distorted and unserviceable mess before throwing them to the ground and piling into my adversary and beating him to a pulp.

Mam wasn't best pleased and had to pay to get me another pair. To my shame I did the same thing again some weeks later.

On joining secondary school I was made aware of someone called 'The Cock of the School'. Before anyone gets totally the wrong idea of what kind of story I am about to tell, the cock of the school meant the best fighter in the school. I also found that there was also a sort of unofficial set of league tables. Cock of the class, Cock of that

39

particular year, and the ultimate accolade of Cock of the school. I was somewhere mid-table.

Girls had no such system or league table, but when they fought, they were breathtaking. Anything was allowed. It was fabulous to watch. A lot of scratching and hair-tugging was involved. When they rolled around on the floor we usually got a brief but wonderful view of their knickers. Certainly something that brightened our day!

Dad taught me that if a fight became inevitable, then the best course of action was to make sure to get the first punch in and to make sure it was a good one. Give your opponent no warning by the usual pushing and posturing.

Someone would taunt me and I would try and avoid them, if they pressed on further I would tell them to go and ....well you get the picture! If they still persisted or 'fronted me up' then WHACK. I would land one straight on the point of their nose, usually making it resemble a squashed tomato. Fight over! This served me well.

One particular day a stocky, thick-set, lad from a year below me started taunting me. I went through all the stages as described above before – WHACK. Indeed his nose opened up a treat. Instead of it ending the fight, he just wiped away the snot and the blood with his sleeve and barelled into me. He wasn't particularly fast; he was just persistent. I rained punches in on him and it made little difference. Finally he wore me out and knocked seven bells out of me. He then helped me up, shook my hand and walked away. Totally bizarre!

Fortunately, in the fifth year, as a senior and studying for exams I was given a bit more room. I was looked upon as almost an adult. This didn't mean that the fighting stopped. A whole new reason for being picked on emerged outside of school.

There have always been thugs and idiots, and probably always will be, but the fact I stayed on at school and studied for my 'O' Levels made some lads think I had airs and graces. They mistakenly thought I looked down on them. An astounding assumption, I came from a poor family and was brought up to think myself no better or worse than anyone.

I don't know if it was the 'book learning' or a natural form of wit taught to me by Dad, but I became good at talking myself out of situations. Most situations I could reason myself out of, usually by massaging the ego of whoever was being difficult to me at the time. A calm demeanour and the odd minor compliment extricated me out of some quite sticky and confrontational situations. Occasionally there was no other course of action but to do a berzerk on them and try and land a few telling punches before legging it. I usually just avoided the watering holes where these Neanderthals gathered.

I had better things to occupy my mind – girls!

1960s – Bedtime

I never minded bedtime. Sitting downstairs in my pyjamas watching TV with a cup of cocoa, then time for bed. I would say all my goodnights and resign myself to the night's comforts and the trip up the stairs to another land. The climb up the stairs and getting into bed was no chore. A hot water bottle in winter. A warm, thick Eiderdown on the bed. Warmth had a certain weight in those days. No lightweight, nylon-filled duvets for us! A couple of blankets and an Eiderdown and the cozy nest was formed.

I had a bedside lamp. I would sit up in bed reading my book. I would charge my mind with adventures from the pages of the adventure book I was reading, until Mam came upstairs and told me to turn off the light and go to sleep. My head would be filled with stories from the pages of the book. I would wait until I heard the door at the bottom of the stairs click shut before getting out my torch. There was always a comic to be read beneath the blankets in rebelliousness.

I had one of those torches that had a little disc in the end of it. When turned, it placed a coloured lens in front of the bulb. It would shine Red, Green, Amber and Blue. In the grey drabness of the dark room the colours shone rainbow bright and excited my mind. The whole of the room became an imaginary playground of the mind that was backlit by the primary colours of the torch. I would imagine everything from remote galaxies to the hues of a summer's garden.

Then drowsiness would begin to overtake me.

Once I lay my head on my pillow I could look out over the surface of the bed and imagine the folds of the blankets and the Eiderdown to be the fields and the rolling hills of some imagined landscape. I would picture myself in a log cabin, looking out through the windows over the landscape. I would imagine that just down in the bottom of the valley was a lake. A lake that was just mine alone. Viewing this perfection of nature, I would drift off to sleep.

In my dreams I would stride through the summer-kissed fields towards the lake. There I would see the carp and the big perch gliding majestically between the lily-pads. I would take my trusty rod and cast my float out across the surface of the pond, and almost instantly the float would glide beneath the surface and I would be playing a wily old perch or a big daddy carp.

This was my small heaven. My elysian landscape. My verdant perfection. Kingfishers were as common as Sparrows and the fields and woods would be alive with birdsong and wildlife. This was my piece of paradise. A secret place known only to me. It waited for me to bring it to life every night. When the light of morning came, it slipped away like Brigadoon to lie in wait for this pilgrim to bless it with his feet when night time came again.

My bedroom was my cave. My refuge and sanctuary from the world's realities and mundane happenings. It was where I felt safe. My little bed was everything from a car to a Roman chariot. An ocean for my ship to sail across to the landscape of an alien planet. During the hours of daylight my bed had more earthly purposes and imaginings such as these. It was only when night fell when it truly came to life. Heaven was the surface of a blanket, and its clouds the fluffy Eiderdown.

Even to this day I know this landscape. It lies untouched. Its virgin fields lie ready to be walked. The old Carp and Perch still glide there in their watery domains. It exists, ready for when my tired and wearied mind needs its safe and gentle meadows. When I crave those times when the world was far simpler and love was like a torrent. A safe but heady torrent that carried you in its arms along the river, to the ocean of peace.

~Peace~

Oh aching feet and wearied mind
that in their desperation seek
the gentle pastures green.
I beg you not forget
the paths that lead you there
Youth is but a concept bare
and years are but a lie.
You are there. Be not a fool
Do not deny the inner child.
That says to you
'Be still'
The world may scream
its fetid song
into your wearied ears.
Hold true!
Keep faith oh weary heart
and see the colours
once again.
Love is but a dream away
and colours never die.

D. Hayes

My Grandad

This story is a difficult one to write. So many issues with it are still like thorns piercing my heart. I can only hope that I do justice to this memory and describe it, warts and all.

Grandad was my personal hero. Some of the prized possessions I have of his are his medals and two of his soldier's pay books. Each weekly pay entry giving the location of where he was.

Fred Hulse was a veteran of World War 1. A member of The Lancashire Fusiliers. His discharge papers state that he was 5ft 5 and a quarter inches tall, of fresh complexion and had served three years and fifty-nine days with the colours. He was invalided out because a trench mortar had put nine pieces of shrapnel into his chest and shoulder. Seven the doctors removed, but two were deemed to be too close to his heart, so he carried them with him to the grave. He was singularly the most influential person of my young and formative days.

As a young child I couldn't say grandfather – all I could say was the father bit. It stuck. Much to the confusion of anyone who didn't know us I would refer to him as 'mi father'.

He told me that the army had taught him how to march and that he had never forgotten it. As a kid he would take me out with him and he would walk the legs off me. A bit of a walk to him was maybe ten miles. I had a toy rifle. He would show me all the moves he had learned in the army and say things like 'slope arms' and 'stand easy'. I lapped it all up.

For all the horror and death he must have witnessed he was the kindest, sweetest, gentlest most patient man I have ever met – and he loved me to bits. He would call me 'my little bohemian boy', to this day I have no idea why, but it was said with love. He bought me a little chair. I still have it. It has a picture of a little Dutch boy and girl on it. He bought me my first watch and, of course, he gave me his medals.

He also taught me some of the old army songs (the clean ones of course). One song he sang to me had the line in it 'if you want to see the private, we know where he is, we know where he is, we know where he is. He's hanging on the old barbed wire.' It was only many, many years later I saw a picture in a museum on the outskirts of Mons of a soldier in a grotesque death pose, entangled in the barbed wire on a battlefield. I made my excuses and said, 'I need to pop outside for a smoke.' It was actually to have a weep in private. I thought to myself how easily that could have been him.

When I was around thirteen he fell ill. Mam used to visit him daily in hospital. She would come back and tell me, 'He is asking when his little soldier was going to visit him.' It was summer, there were fish to catch, trees to climb; there was loads of time. 'Mi Father' will be out soon and we will go walking again – it never happened.

Three days later Mam came home and I could see that she had been crying. She said to me that she had been there when he passed away and that his last words were, 'Where's my little soldier?' It destroyed me!

I ran from the house with tears streaming down my face. I just ran and ran – down all the lanes where we walked. I don't know if, in my crazed mind, I was looking for him. I lay in a field of long grass and wept for hours. All the time with Mam's words echoing in my head.

People flippantly ask the question, 'If you could bring someone back for an hour to talk to, who would it be?' With me the answer would be a simple one. It would be him. I would beg his forgiveness. Of course, this doesn't happen in real life – I just hope there is an after-life to be able to put right the damage – the damage to us both.

Stand to Attention

"Stand to attention soldier"
My Grandfather's gentle voice spoke
I saluted him as I had been shown
"At ease," he spoke again
Then he pinned his medals to my shirt
One by one, those shining discs
Almost holy to me
The proof of what I knew
He was my hero
The game over I went to hand them back
No my little one, they are yours
Disbelief, the responsibility overwhelmed me
I looked into his eyes but saw no joke
No laughter, only love
"Grandfather," I asked
"Is it OK for soldiers to cry?"

David Hayes

1967 – Wildlife

Although born to the cobbled streets and gas lamps of a mining town, the countryside and all it held was like a drug to me. It ran through my veins. I knew the places to fish and where to see which kind of bird, heralding each visiting summer migrant to our shores and imagining their journeys from distant lands. I took with me no notepad and pencil. They were written on the pages of my heart.

Most of this wisdom had been passed to me by Uncle Jimmy. A man so at one with nature I felt sure he could walk through a field of long grass and leave no tracks! He was my Gandalf – my own private wizard. He taught me how to fish for pike and big perch in the lakes and ponds. He told me the names of all the different types of ducks and waders, and how to identify them by their calls. He explained to me all about the noise that the secretive snipe makes. He called it 'drumming'. He explained that they made the sound by passing air through their feathers. It is a sound that I still find haunting and evocative.

It is my opinion that once you discover the wonders of nature and the joys of all that the wilderness has to offer, you are never bored. A simple walk with a pair of binoculars, or a few hours spent fishing is enough for a lifetime. Even in winter it has a majesty that can capture the imagination. Identifying the different animal tracks. Trying to glean what visitors you had to your garden in the night by their tracks in the pristine snow.

One evening, Uncle Jimmy sent for me and he said 'Do you want to see something very special David?' I nodded eagerly. He always knew the secret places. The places that only he and nature knew existed. 'I'll ask your Mam if you can stay out late,' he said. Mam agreed as I didn't have school the next day.

We headed off towards a copse that was in a remote corner of some arable farming land. We followed a footpath round to it. It was on the edge of a bigger wood, but was slightly separated from it. It was near the perimeter of a small lake. I wondered how on earth he had found this unremarkable looking place, and what we were doing there. We entered the copse. We squatted down behind a fallen tree. He told me to sit very quietly and not to shuffle around or speak. In front of us, and about fifteen yards away was what I took to be a fox hole.

That night, as youth coursed through my veins, I felt eternal. I sat and waited for the wonders to unfold on that cold, damp night. At last they emerged, sniffing the air – aware of us I am sure, but taking a risk. Almost knowing instinctively we meant no harm. They were badgers. I screamed inwardly with the thrill of it all. This was like a nature programme on TV, but we had been invited into the studios for a command performance. My first sight of a live Badger!

The croaking and squealing of the adolescent cubs as they rough and tumbled near us. So near us we heard the dried grasses sizzle with their play – like tinkers' fires on a cold night. A host of angels could have descended and been no more splendid to me than the sweet privacy of Mother Nature's secrets that were unfolded before my eyes. They gladdened this country boy's heart and set his pulse a-racing.

I cannot say how long we gazed upon this amazing spectacle. I suppose it must have been an hour. Time meant nothing to us when confronted with such wonders. They moved away from us and began to forage. When we were sure they were far enough away, we crept away like thieves. My youth, my future, my present and my past had

50

all crystallized into one perfect frosty, moonlit evening. I returned home unaware of the ache in my bones, but instead I revelled in the spring that had returned to my steps.

On the orders and advice of Uncle Jimmy, I afforded them their privacy and didn't venture forth to view them again. The temptation to do so was very strong, but a trust had been bestowed upon me – almost a sacred bond. I knew that there would be many other nights and other games afoot, when we ventured out to peep inside Mother Nature's secret chambers and witness her and her creatures screened from our sight, but revealed to us in thrilling glimpses as the veil lifted for a few precious moments. Mother Nature was often at her finest when bedecked in her night clothes. The mysteries she held seemed more piquant than when she wore her bright summer dresses of daytime. She was beautiful whenever you saw her. She was gentle but cruel. Happy but unforgiving. She was life itself.

My Place Within Nature

When the sun shines
it is too precious to waste.
When the rains come
they feed the ground.
When the snow falls
it cleanses all.
When the night comes
it lays to rest
all my dreams.
When my time comes
I will have done all I can.
Bathe me with your sunshine
and bless me with your tears.
Cover my shame with your frosts
and bury my dreams in your darkness.
When my time has come
to be the care-worn angel
Nature has planned,
and takes me to my rest,
I will be amongst Nature.
Look for me
in the quick glance
of a Fox.
Look for me
in the twitch
of a rabbit's whiskers.
Look for me
in the song of a blackbird.
Look for me
in the petals
of a humble daisy.
For there,
and only there
will you find my heart.

D. Hayes

1967 – Young Guns

I would be around thirteen. It was the summer holidays and my friends and I had decided to head off to the park. When we arrived the place was empty, which was fairly uncommon. Usually the place was bustling with kids, mothers with prams and old folks sitting on the benches getting a little fresh air. We gravitated towards the park keeper's building to find Old Jack there (as everyone knew him). As young kids we found Old Jack rather intimidating. He was treated almost as some kind of bogey man. If you were in the park and doing something you shouldn't have been, someone would say, 'Jack's coming' and we would all run. As we grew older we just found him to be a kindly old man who just stood no nonsense.

We asked him if we could buy tickets for the putting green. A little ten hole pitch where you hired a putter and a ball, and he gave you a score card and a pencil. He said we could as long as we didn't mind taking a brush and sweeping off the leaves from the pitch and setting all the flags out. All of a sudden it had lost its attraction. This involved work!

One of our gang, a lad called Michael, said, 'Can we have a go at bowling?' Jack looked at him as if he had asked for his daughter's hand in marriage. Jack's bowling green was his pride and joy. It was immaculately kept with its striped pattern and spotlessly clean gullies. A couple of local teams used his green as their home green, and he was fiercely jealous of his hallowed turf.

He said to us, 'Let's look at your shoes.' We all had tennis shoes or baseball boots on (this was before trainers were invented). Jack said, 'Those will do.' He took us into the bowls room and chose us a couple of bowls each and a jack. He also handed me a rubber mat. He took us on to the green and explained that the bowls had a bias. That meant that they ran in a curve. He explained all about finger peg and thumb peg (which meant the way you held the bowl with the bias towards your thumb or your little finger). He also explained that this was crown green bowls, which meant that the centre of the green was raised a little. We suddenly realised that this wasn't as effortless as it seemed.

He threw down the mat and gracefully bowled the jack so it came to rest around six feet short of the diagonally opposite corner. His first bowl landed some ten feet short but his second bowl landed to within a couple of feet. So, that's how you did it!

Our first few games were terrible. We hadn't got the hang of finger peg and thumb peg. Some bowls were almost in opposite corners, but soon we picked up the hang of it and were managing to get them within a decent distance. We enjoyed it so much that we came back again every day. After a couple of weeks, we noticed a few old chaps turning up and sitting on the park benches that surrounded the green. Day on day the crowd grew until we had as many as thirty or so all watching us. They actually began to applaud and said such things as 'Good wood there young 'un.' and 'Good use of finger peg.' It became exciting. We had fans!!

One day, as we were leaving the green to polite applause, a couple of men approached us. One said, 'Can I have a chat with you lads?' He saw the look on our faces and he laughed. 'Don't panic – you aren't in any trouble,' he said. He then asked us our ages. When we said that we were thirteen his face dropped. The man accompanying him mumbled 'shit' under his breath.

He then went on to tell us that he was the secretary of the local British Legion bowling team. He told us that he wanted us in his reserve side with a view to bringing us into the main side. We were gobsmacked. The Legion had one of the top sides in the district. A few had gone on to bowl nationally. It was like a scout from Manchester United had approached us and asked us to sign papers. Then came the crushing disappointment. We had to be sixteen. His friend looked through the rule book and that was the rule. No if's, no but's.

We carried on bowling for the rest of the summer and into the autumn; then the greens were closed. We never went again the following year. We had moved on to new adventures. An old motorbike being one of them. Waiting two or three years to join a team was like asking us to serve a prison sentence. Life had more immediate pleasures. We consoled ourselves by saying such things as, 'It's an old man's game anyway.'

Sad really! Our span of attention was short in our early teens. Life was measured in seconds not years. Now, if I discover a talent that I possess, I try and develop it and nurture it to become even better, but that said I now don't have motorbikes to tinker with or girls to chase after (both of which proved to be expensive in later years!).

Apart from being a pretty decent darts player in my 20s, bowling was the only sport I like to think I showed promise in.

I often wonder what would have happened had we carried on. Would we now be the subject of one of those photographs hanging on the Legion wall? Would it be us jubilantly holding aloft some trophy or other? I know a couple of local men who went on to make a very good living out of playing bowls in tournaments all over the country. Makes you wonder!

1960s – Christmas Morning

These days Christmas just seems to come and go. Although I love the day and seeing the joy etched into kid's faces as they open their presents and get the gifts they had wished for, it all seems a bit contrived, expensive and plastic.

When I think back to Christmas, I remember it as a magical time. It started when we brought down the tree and the other bits and pieces and festooned the house with the decorations we had kept for years. Some of them looked a little tired, but this just added to the mystique. It was part of our own private tradition. The old decorations were like old friends who came out to greet us every year with their tired but honest smiles. Baubles were brought out reverently and gently placed on the tree. Each one had its own story and memories. Then went on the Christmas lights and the tinsel.

Once the tree was dressed, we would turn off the house lights and switch on the Christmas tree lights. There was a chorus of comments from, 'Oooo isn't it lovely' to 'The best in the street I reckon.' Dad would sit at the piano and play a couple of carols and we would all sing. This may seem a little bit 'Waltons', but it was all part of the magic that Mam and Dad wove for us. We had little or no money but we all had each other, and it was more than enough.

On Christmas Eve I would go to bed way too excited to rest, but eventually the sandman would do his work and I would be off to sleep. When I awoke I would see little gifts in a stocking at the foot of my bed. It was the best of all magic. I would imagine Father

Christmas magically appearing to leave these gifts just for me. I felt like a king.

I would descend the stairs at some early, ungodly hour to show Mam and Dad what Santa had left, and then Mam would say, 'Come and see what else he has left you.' One year it was something big propped up against the kitchen wall and covered in a blanket. I whisked off the blanket and found a bike. It had three speed gears and a saddle bag – it was amazing! Years later I found out that Dad had bought it from one of my cousins as he had outgrown it and had replaced it with a racing bike.

There were the annuals such as *The Beezer* and *The Beano*, A chocolate smokers' set (imagine giving a kid THAT today!) and some money donated by kindly aunts and uncles to spend in the shops.

Christmas was so all-embracing you could almost reach out and feel it. There was also the delicious smell of the Christmas dinner drifting in from the kitchen. Mam would warn us all, 'Don't eat any sweets until after your dinner – I don't want you to spoil your appetite.' So we would all busy ourselves with our presents or the TV, all the time salivating like spaniels before being fed.

When it was time for dinner Mam would bring out the turkey. Apparently she had been putting aside a bit of money all year in a Christmas club so we could afford to push the boat out a little. The turkey was magnificent. All bronzed and beautiful with crispy skin accompanied by little cocktail sausages and veg of every kind in bowls around it. Nothing since has ever tasted as good as Mam's Christmas dinner.

After we had eaten, we would lounge around on the chairs and sofa like walruses, blissfully full and wanting for nothing. After a while it was time for games. Usually it was charades where we had to guess the names of films and songs from little slips of paper that Dad had pre-written on bits of folded paper and placed in an old biscuit tin for us to choose. Sometimes we played Monopoly or Snakes and Ladders. Then it was TV time.

If the weather was nice we would go outside and meet up with our friends and show our presents and all play together. Everywhere was quiet. Very little background traffic or factory noise. The whole world seemed to be a playground. As it grew dusk we would be called in for our tea, then it was TV time. There were the films, things like 'It's a Wonderful World' and 'National Velvet' and the Christmas specials such as *Morecambe and Wise*. Whilst watching TV we would re-abuse our stomachs by munching on sweets.

All too soon it was bedtime and we were packed off to bed. Then it was Mam and Dad's time to relax.

1965 – The Wood Yard

Most kids of our generation had some kind of job to earn a bit of spending money. A couple of friends of mine had a job at a local wood yard. The owner of the yard would cut up old floor boards and other similar timbers to make bundles of firewood. My mates introduced me to him as one of his lads didn't want the job any more as he had landed a paper round. So he gave me a job.

There was a big circular saw at the end of a big shed. We weren't allowed anywhere remotely near it for obvious reasons. It was actually big enough to cut one of us in half. He would saw the wood into blocks on this saw, to a length of around eight inches long, and these would be piled up alongside the saw. He had two bigger lads who chopped this up into the actual firewood with hand axes. This is where we came in. He had three metal clamp affairs. They were two semi-circular jaws with a handle alongside. When you pulled the handle towards you, the jaws would close together into a perfect circle. You would open the jaws, place the firewood inside them and pull the handle. This would clamp the loose wood into a tight bundle. And a piece of wire would be twisted around it. These wires were in a box alongside and ready cut to length. Alongside each clamp would be a big hessian sack for the firewood bundles to be placed inside.

I loved this shed. He had an old-fashioned pot-bellied stove with a pipe that exited through the apex of the roof. This was our central heating on cold nights. You would hear it roaring up the stove pipe, and the sides of the stove would actually glow cherry-red once it got going properly. The smell of burning wood is so aromatic and homely. I love it to this day. The smell of the freshly cut wood and the oil used to lubricate the wood clamps would all mix together with the wood smoke. Add to this the smell of the pipe tobacco that he smoked, and there you had the constituents of the unique aroma of that wood shed. I would love to smell it again. It would be so evocative of those days.

You were paid on the number of sacks that you filled. He would pick up the sacks and give them a shake by bouncing them on the ground. This would settle and compact the bundles so you could fit more in. He knew all the tricks we could play. He made sure he got his money's worth out of us. This makes him sound unkind. He wasn't. He was a happy chap who worked during the day as a plumber, then came to his shed after work to earn a bit more money, and 'To get from under the wife's feet' as he put it.

We would work Monday to Friday, a couple of hours each night, and Friday was pay day. He would count up the number of sacks we had each filled and we would be paid accordingly. I would earn anything between two and six to four bob on a good week. I remember my first week. I must have been very enthusiastic and taken no breaks. I earned three and six (17.5 pence). It was a fortune to me. As was the custom, we headed off to the newsagents to do some damage to the penny chews counter.

My two mates were 'bagging-up' on *Black Jacks*, *Fruit Salads*, and *Flying Saucers*, but I had my eye on a big bar of Cadbury's Chocolate. I bought the huge block of chocolate and bought a few penny tray sweets. I had sixpence left in my pocket. We headed off home through the streets that were bathed in the blue-green light of the street-lamps. It was a very gentle glow, and gave the streets an ethereal, other-worldly, soft tone. This was before the advent of those depressing orange hued street lights we have today.

On arriving home, everyone was watching TV. Dad was in his chair and my two sisters were on the sofa. Mam was on the other chair and she was knitting. When I walked in through the door, Mam asked me how I had gone on, and asked what it felt like being a working man. This sounded wonderful – 'A Working Man', how grown up I felt. I told her that I had earned three and six, but still had some left. She told me to come into the kitchen and sit at the table and she would make me some toast and a cup of tea.

As the kettle was brewing I took the big bar of chocolate from inside my coat where I had been hiding it. I handed it to her and said 'I've bought you a present Mam. I know you like chocolate'. She grabbed hold of me and hugged me so hard that I actually farted. She thanked me and went into the front room and said to everyone 'Look what our David has bought me'. Dad gave me a proud smile, and I heard a chorus of 'Awww bless him' from my sisters.

Mam waited until I had finished my toast and tea and then brought out the chocolate. We all had a couple of squares each, then the rest was put away in the cupboard for other evenings. All that week she bought me little things like comics and caps for my cap gun. If all was added up I probably came out well in profit. I don't know whether my brief attendance of Sunday School had an impact. Perhaps I remembered the words, 'Cast thy bread upon the waters'. This time it really did work!

Early to Mid 1960s – My Two Sisters and Their Boyfriends

As was the custom in those days, any boys that my two sisters had been going out with for a few weeks would be summoned to appear at our house (or Gestapo Headquarters as my eldest sister called it) to be vetted by Mam and Dad. One particularly memorable occasion springs to mind.

It was an excruciatingly embarrassing ordeal for my eldest sister and her amorous suitor, but to me it was hilarious! Out came the best china from on top of the wardrobe. All the dust and dead spiders were shaken out of the tea cups and they were washed and prepared for the forthcoming 'trial-by-fire'.

On the arrival of the happy couple, Dad adopted the quiet but strong demeanour, whilst Mam was animated and accommodating. Her voice subtly changed to a weird, semi-refined accent somewhere between 'speaking proper' as my Nanna would say, and her normal, working-class, northern accent. She made a valiant attempt at class and refinement by saying, 'Would you care for a fondant fancy?' Unfortunately, she then let herself down by following it up with 'They are proper lovely.' I had been warned by Mam to 'sit quietly' which was followed up with, 'I don't want you showing us all up.' I thought to myself, 'I wouldn't dream of it Mam – you are doing brilliantly on your own!'

Dad was pretending to read the Daily Mirror just to rack up the tension, before finally folding it up, slowly – then with a theatrical sigh he placed it meticulously into the magazine rack. His opening gambit to the ashen-faced boyfriend was, 'Do I know your parents?'

You could see the poor thing squirming in his suede shoes and struggling for an answer. 'I..erm...well..erm...I don't know Mr Hayes...sir...sorry.'

Dad then tried to leave it all to Mam. He had taken part in the 'three ringed circus' as he used to call these particular events.

In this particular instance, Mam looked at Dad and gave him one of her 'Well say something else for God's sake' looks. Dad answered the look with his 'What do you want me to say?' look.

Mam desperately entreated my Dad to ask the boy some more questions. 'Ask him some questions, Seth,' she said, 'don't just sit there. We don't know who he is – he might be an axe murderer for all we know.'

The prospective boyfriend's eyes were now as wide as saucers – 'God this is great' I thought to myself – they are now accusing him of being an axe murderer!

Dad rolled his eyes, turned to the boy and said, 'Are you an axe murderer lad?'

The traumatized boyfriend couldn't even muster up an answer. He just vigorously shook his head from side to side.

This was the moment I seized the golden opportunity by asking, 'Hey Mam, can I have a Fondant Fancy?'

Her eyes flashed a warning signal that said, 'Don't play me up you little bugger.' She frostily handed one to me on a garish Crown Devon side plate from the dinner service. On one previous occasion she handed me a fork to eat it with (I think she had seen it happen at my cousin's wedding and thought it ever so refined). I said, 'Thanks Mam' before skewering the entire fondant fancy on the end of the fork and eating it like a toffee apple. She had learned her lesson and I was allowed to eat the cake with my fingers.

If the poor, long-suffering boyfriend could put up with this debacle, he must be keen, I thought to myself.

Some hour or so later (which probably felt like a year to them), my sister and her poor, traumatised boyfriend made their excuses to leave as they had a dance or some such to attend. They were walked to the door and heralded on their way by Mam with such remarks as, 'Lovely to meet you' and 'Don't be late back' and yet again she spoiled her refinement by finishing off the sentence with 'our Lilian'.

The door finally closed and Dad took the opportunity to break wind as he had been holding it in for half an hour. This was the bugle call that told us all that we were back in working class mode. 'Roll on the next one' I thought to myself – 'I like fondant fancies'.

1960s – A Breath of Fresh Air

Sometimes I miss the old two up, two down terraced house I was born in – I was *actually* born in it. Upstairs in the front bedroom. It was No 5 in a row of twelve. It was a community in the true sense. Everyone knew and helped everyone else.

We had open back yards with no separating walls, which helped to further foster the community feel to it. It was no unusual thing to find your neighbour had brought in your washing if you were out and it had started to rain. Similarly, they would put a shovelful of coal on the fire for you if you were out to keep the fire in for you on cold days.

Insurance men and the rent man would call. The money and the book would be left on the sideboard and the front door would be unlocked (or even wide open if it was a warm day) and he would walk in and collect his money and sign your book. There really was trust. Any shifty looking strangers would be spotted immediately and a close eye would be kept on them. For the first ten years of my life I thought the whole world was like this!

At the back of the house, a path of around fifteen yards or so led to a toilet at the bottom of the yard. The toilet door opened outwards and it had no lock on it. It was said you soon learned to whistle or sing a song to inform others of your occupation of the space. The door also had a four inch gap at the bottom of it. I assume this was for ventilation purposes! Hanging behind the door would be ready cut squares of newspaper with a hole punched in the corner and threaded onto a string. The reason for these being quite obvious.

I don't know what it is about sitting on the toilet and being able to hear the sparrows chirping outside, and feeling a breeze blowing around your ankles from the gap under the door that made me feel good, but it did. It felt somehow natural and right. There was none of the 'I would give that five minutes if I were you' problems. It was almost like being in the open, and any unpleasant odours dissipated in seconds. On a breezy day, instantly! If someone was occupying the toilet I could walk a few yards and use Nanna's.

Winter brought its problems, though. If you suspected a heavy frost, you had to put a paraffin heater in there to keep the pipes from freezing. A paraffin lamp was often enough. It kept the temperature just above freezing point. Also, there was no light in there, so you had to take a torch. Either that or just take aim and hope! Our toilet was quite roomy. I don't know what it had been before being a flush toilet – perhaps a small storage building. There was enough room in there to hang a big tin bath from a strong hook on the wall.

The tin bath made me think of a wicked idea: a plot to cause some mischief. I had been outside in the back yard one dark winter's evening when I popped my head round the back door and told Mam I was going round to Nanna's house. What I actually did was sneak inside the toilet and hid myself behind the big tin bath and waited. After about fifteen minutes I heard the sound of feet on the cinder pathway, heard the latch on the door click and saw the door open and close through the crack between the bath and the wall. I heard a cough and recognised it as my eldest sister's.

I waited until she was settled and heard the tinkling water sound and then let out a long, mournful wailing noise and started banging the sides of the bath. She screamed like someone about to be murdered and I heard the door being flung open. By the light of the moon I could see the streak of pee leading from the toilet to our back door. I was absolutely helpless with laughter and quite literally rolling around on the floor.

Dad came flying out of the back door holding a poker and was ready to do battle with the intruder when he saw me and laughed. 'It's only our David buggering about,' he announced to the anxiously waiting family. Everyone found it hilarious (apart from my sister of course).

Stupidly, I tried this trick again a couple of weeks later, but this time (and unluckily for me) it was Dad. He heard me let out the wail, and the next thing I knew the bath had been jammed hard against the wall by Dad's foot. He then proceeded to bang nine bells out of the sides of the bath before slinging the bath, with me in it, through the toilet door. Dazed and crawling out of the bath, I saw Dad standing and the toilet door open. He said, 'Let me have a pee in peace you little bugger', then he slammed the door behind himself.

I also remember it being a place where my sister went to have a crafty cigarette. Even though Mam and Dad knew she smoked, it was something you just didn't do in front of them – even though they both smoked themselves. It was a matter of respect.

Another game I devised involved clambering on to the roof of the toilet to wait in ambush. It was easy to do. I climbed onto the bin and then hoisted myself on to the adjoining wall, and then on to the toilet roof. There was a gap at the top of the toilet door of about an inch. Just wide enough to fit the muzzle of a water pistol through it. I picked my targets carefully though. If I saw it was Mam or Dad I didn't do anything. My sisters were legitimate prey though!

I remember one bonfire night. Our houses had a small piece of waste ground behind them, and then there were the backs of the newer council houses and their back yards. I had let off all my fireworks early and I saw the people in the council house, that was back to back with us, come out to light their fireworks. I climbed onto the toilet roof and had a ringside seat to their far superior fireworks party.

The house was primitive with all the hot water coming from a small gas boiler on the kitchen wall, no bath and an outside toilet, but so what! It was where my world was. All our wonderful neighbours and the kids in my little gang. When I was eleven we moved into a council house a mile away and they pulled down our little house. It felt like we had moved to Mars. No one knew anyone around them, except maybe the next door neighbours. It felt so cold and impersonal. It took a few years to readjust.

1968 – Abscess

I hated the dentist. He was the 'old-school' type of dentist, and when I went for fillings he didn't numb the gum, oh no, – he just drilled away merrily and picked at the cavity with that little metal hook of his. This had the effect of making sweat pump from my forehead and my fingers dig into the chair arm until my knuckles were white with the effort. In many ways it scarred me (as well as scared me) for years afterwards.

One morning I noticed a swelling in my top gum, just below my nose, and a throbbing pain that accompanied it. I had no choice – I had to go to Dr Death as I called him. As I waited in his waiting room for the call, I started to look around the place. Perhaps it was to take my mind off what was about to happen.

He had a lovely old Art Nouveau bookcase with the words 'Books, like friends, should be few and well chosen' in what I later discovered was Charles Rennie Mackintosh font. That bookcase (if it still exists) is probably worth a fortune now – especially if it was an original piece by the great man himself (Can you tell I am a fan of his work?).

Soon came the call 'David Hayes please'. I walked into his torture chamber. He waved his hand towards his chair and barked at me, 'Sit down'. I did as I was told. He took a look inside my mouth and said, 'Tsk, an abscess. That's going to hurt'. That filled me full of joy as you can well imagine! 'Can't you do anything?' I asked him. He told me that I just had to wait until it burst, and then I was to come back. His final parting shot was 'Buy some Aspirins'.

It took around two days to finally burst. I didn't hardly eat or sleep. No matter what I took the pain was there constantly. Mam had the idea of telling me to swill neat whisky around my gums as the alcohol might numb the pain. After a while I was unpleasantly tipsy and feeling very sorry for myself. Mam said 'I didn't mean drink it, just swill it round and spit it out'. Perhaps it would have been better if she had explained that first?

When it finally did burst I had been quite literally pacing up and down the kitchen crying with the pain. I suddenly felt something pop inside my mouth and a foul taste ensued. The pain left me almost instantly. Mam told me not to swallow it and to rinse out my mouth. I asked her if I should use the whisky again (well I had to try didn't I?) and she said to me, 'Don't try it on. No, use warm water from the kettle and a little salt'. I rinsed out my mouth and another appointment with 'Dr Death' was made for two days later.

I arrived once again at his surgery and he greeted me with, 'I take it that it burst, did it?', I nodded at him. He then said 'Perhaps you will take better care of your teeth and come and see me more often?' What stopped me from telling him to sod off and calling him a sarcastic old git, I don't know. I didn't think it wise as aforesaid 'old git' was about to start fiddling around in my mouth. He took a look at it and said, 'Yes, that has to come out.' My spirits sank.

He told me that he was going to inject my gum to numb it (which was a huge relief as I did wonder whether he was just going to yank it out of my face without anything) but he followed it up by saying that the nerves were probably coated by the remnants of the abscess wall and, as he euphemistically put it, I might feel a little discomfort.

His assistant interlocked her fingers and clamped them around my forehead and they began. He was right. It was 'uncomfortable' to buggery! I would say that it was like having no anaesthetic at all. I screamed out a long, gurgling 'Aaaaargggggggg' but mercifully, quickly, it was over. He said to me that I looked a little pale (hardly surprising!), and just when I thought he cared a little, he followed it up with, 'I don't want you fainting on me, I have enough to do without that.' The fact that it was free was at least one small relief.

Since then I have indeed looked after my teeth and have found a wonderful dentist. Everything is pain-free these days, and there is even a little TV set over the chair where I can watch 'Good Morning Britain' whilst having a filling, or a crown replaced. Even now though, when I sit in the waiting room, the whine of that drill still makes me nervous!

1960s – Going To The Temp

In the sixties (and even into the seventies and later) we had establishments that were called Temperance Bars. One particular local one was known to us as Hall's. It was run by a nice old lady by the name of Mrs Hall (or at least I assume that was her name!). There was a Mr Hall who occasionally made an appearance but, largely speaking, it was usually Mrs Hall.

Temperance Bars came into existence in the late 19th century as an alternative to the pub. The Temperance Movement was a fairly powerful one and attempted to get people to 'sign the pledge' and abstain from alcoholic drinks. I suppose it was a kind of American prohibition but it was optional (and the alternative wasn't run by the mob!)

Our particular temperance bar (or The Temp as we knew it) was a sight to behold, (though little did we realise or appreciate it at the time). It was decked out inside with wood panelling and an actual pub-style bar. There were bench seats around the perimeter and a couple of cast iron pub tables. Above the panelling the walls were tiled with green and white art nouveau styled tiles and the floor was a sort of chequerboard pattern with alternate black and white floor tiles. The old gas lamps were still there, but had been converted to electricity.

As you pushed open the old Victorian door with its etched glass panels, a small bell above the door would tinkle to announce your arrival. The first thing that hit you was the smell. It was so hard to describe; it was delicious. There were Christmas-like overtones of cinnamon, the intoxicating smell of vanilla and a whole cacophony of fruity mid tones emanating from the lovely drinks and cordials. I am salivating just thinking about it! It also sold sweets and crisps and had a freezer with ice cream and lollies.

As you walked up to the counter, Mrs Hall would say, 'What can I get you luv?' This is when the quandary started, what to choose! There was a drinks menu on the wall. They had Dandelion and Burdock (not the fizzy bottled stuff, REAL Dandelion and Burdock), Sarsaparilla, Ginger Beer, something called Black Beer, Cream Soda, Vimto, Blackcurrant, the list went on and on. One of my favourites was Sarsaparilla. Even then, once you had chosen, you had a further choice to make. Mrs Hall would ask, 'Do you want it still or fizzy luv?' I usually took mine still.

On cold winter's days we would set off early and call in on our way to school. They made hot Vimto. Just the ticket to warm up frozen little fingers on those cold mornings. I wore glasses, so as soon as I took a sip from the glass my spectacles would totally fog over, much to the amusement of my pals. I would drink my Vimto and stumble out like a blind person. My glasses would instantly clear once the freezing air hit them.

The Temp wasn't just a shop that sold drinks, it was a meeting place. A common expression was 'I'll meet you at the temp'. You would arrange to meet your pals there and you could enjoy a nice drink whilst you waited for them to show up. You could stay in there all day if you liked, as long as you kept on buying stuff! If you didn't, Mrs Hall would come round to collect the glasses and drop hints like, 'Are you done with that now?' which was her way of saying go away and stop cluttering up my tables. If you liked a girl, it was the norm to 'take her up the temp' (and yes, I am fully aware that you could make that sound rude).

Our temp closed some time in the mid 70s. It was such a sad sight to see it all boarded up. I drove by there some time in the early 90s. It had all changed. It now had some posh Italian name and seemed to be frequented by the cappuccino and Pannini brigade. I pulled over and went inside to buy a coffee. I almost wept. Everything had gone. It was now a white, sterile, wipe down walls kind of place with awful red plastic chairs and glass tables. I was served by some soulless assistant who looked like she was on minimum wage and would act and serve you accordingly almost in robotic fashion.

I drank my coffee and left the place. I sat in my car for a few moments and just shook my head. The schools I went to were no longer there. The house I was born in was gone with the slum clearances, and now they have taken my temp! I thought to myself that it felt like someone was trying to wipe out my entire childhood as if it had never happened! Had I allowed myself the luxury of it, I could have sat there and had a weep, but I didn't. I shook it off and carried on with my journey.

On still nights, when all the lights are off and the place is dark and empty, I wonder if Mrs Hall walks inside her beloved shop. I wonder if she is still there, wiping down her marble topped counter and filling up her shelves with clean glasses. If you stood outside long enough, would you hear the tinkle of that long since removed door bell and hear the voice of Mrs Hall say in her jolly tones, 'What can I get you luv?' I like to think she is still there amongst her wood panelling and delicious aromas, resplendent in her white pinafore waiting to serve her customers. The alternative is too painful to contemplate.

Winter 1967 – My Sister's House is Haunted?

The winter nights had started drawing in. It was a particularly cold November. Mam was at the sink washing up and I was reading *The Dandy* at the kitchen table. It would be around 6pm in the evening. Without warning our back door flew open, startling everyone in the room. It was my eldest sister. She seemed in a right state! She just kept saying 'I'm moving back home – I'm not going back to that bloody house – no way'.

Mam sat her down with a nice, hot sugary tea (the cure for all traumas) and told her to calm down and speak slowly as she was babbling. She then told us all that her little terraced house was haunted – and what's more, she had physical proof! When we all (in unison) said 'WHAT PROOF?' she told us that she had been flicking a feather duster over the light shade in the middle of her living room ceiling when she spotted a perfect, man-size shoe print right next to it. 'Nobody can walk on the ceiling, Mam,' she said in a tear jerked voice. Mam told her that there was probably a down-to-earth explanation and that she was probably wrong and that it just LOOKED like a footprint. She then said, 'Our David will go back with you and stay with you until Jimmy (her husband) gets home.'

Oh thanks Mam, I thought to myself. Send your twelve-year-old son off into the night with a crazed woman to go and sit in a haunted house for three or four hours, but if Mam said go – you went!

We walked back the mile or so to her house. The wind was blowing through the trees and a full moon was peeping from behind a cloud. You couldn't have scripted it any better. We got to her front door and I said to her, 'Let me go first.' (like I would have been any good if anything had stepped out and said BOO. I would have messed my trousers). I ran inside and fumbled for the light switch and said to her, 'It's okay, you can come in – it's safe.'

I then asked her where this haunted footprint was, just barely keeping the derision out of my voice. She pointed to an area of the ceiling and I looked up and saw it. It really was a perfect shoe-print on the ceiling. Okay, now I was in the realms of stuff I couldn't handle! We both just sat on her couch and never moved until her husband came home and she collapsed into his arms in a flood of tears. I was then left to walk home – on my own. I ran most of the way.

It was many years later and I happened to be out fishing with Jimmy. We got on to the subject of ghosts and such. I said to him, 'That was a funny do, wasn't it – that footprint on your ceiling?'

He grinned widely and said to me, 'Can you keep a secret?'

I said, 'Sure.' He then told me that he and my sister were having a blazing argument. He had just come in from the muddy back yard to get some coal for the fire and, in sheer temper, he had petulantly kicked off his carpet slipper while she was in the kitchen sulking. It made a perfect footprint on the newly painted ceiling. He knew that he dare not mention it as she would throw a hissy fit and make him repaint it.

1968 – The Awakening

The change from child to adolescent is a subtle one. It crept upon me like an assassin. Life began to take on a seriousness, and I began to become far more self-conscious. Education became far more focussed upon, and the teachers discussed with us which career paths we wished to embark upon. I wanted to say that I had my heart set on becoming a teacher, or a civil servant, but that would involve going on to further education, and circumstances dictated that this would not be possible, so I picked the job that my brother-in-law did and said I wanted to be a fitter.

Clothing, before adolescence was merely a functional thing. It kept you warm and dry and covered your nakedness. I became painfully aware that it now had a totally new significance. I was aware that I had what was called an image. The clothes I wore and the music I professed to like would mark me out for the category of friends I would hang around with.

I was far too self-conscious to dress sharply and hang around with the cool kids. All these people knew me. You couldn't just re-invent yourself and suddenly become transformed. All that it would have caused was hilarity had I rocked up to school one day dressed like 'a cool dude'. There was also another factor to consider – poverty. Dad was ill and Mam couldn't work because she had to look after him.

I made a start though – I started to grow my hair. I slowly started to introduce bits of clothing to my ensemble. The first thing to arrive were flared jeans. I expected to be the centre of unwanted attraction, but no one seemed to notice, as everyone else was wearing them too. I think my mate Ivan said, 'Oh flares – about time too!' Apart from that it passed relatively unnoticed. My hair took on weirder styles as it grew, but again, other boys were growing their hair too, so no big deal.

A little later I added a couple of shirts with large, round-ended collars. One solid colour though. I wasn't brave enough for a flowered shirt yet. I think the tank top came a little later. Fishtail Parkas were also quite popular and could be bought at a reasonable price from *The Army and Navy Stores*, so it became my coat of choice. I guess I was a weird mix of a Mod and a Hippie- a Mippie I suppose!

As everyone around me became more and more outrageous, I followed suit, but in a slightly more muted fashion. I eventually became the owner of a few flowered shirts and multi-coloured tank tops, so my image began to take shape. My hair was now past collar length and attracting comments from the older generation such as, 'Get your hair cut, you look like a girl.' So I knew I was on the right track.

I was excruciatingly shy around girls and almost began to fear them in a strange way! They were beginning to develop a very pleasing shape and to look like grown-ups. They also hunted in packs. The gorgeous and iconic ones were the sole domain of the good looking athletes at school, or even older boys who were now working. I suppose we were like the young lions who patrolled the outskirts of the pride looking for stragglers.

Sex began to be bragged about excessively amongst us boys. We lied constantly about what we had been up to. A few had even professed to have 'broken their duck', but this was always viewed with scepticism. We were all lying as well, so it stood to reason that everyone else was. This didn't mean that it didn't increase the pressure, because it did. The hunt for a girlfriend became obsessive!

The girls seemed so demure and in control. I am sure they were suffering just as badly as we were, but in an entirely different way. The two things that they had in their favour were strength in numbers, and the fact that it was the boy's job to approach the girl and expose himself to possible ridicule. A feat I never managed to achieve. I eventually found my first girlfriend in a totally different way.

I became a fifth year at school and stayed on to take my 'O' Levels. I had a pretty unique fifth year class at school. There were four of us boys, and two girls – that was it! We became a clique and hung around together constantly. I ended up going out with one of these girls who became my first love. A story I have covered previously. Thinking back, these were the best days of my life. I have never felt the highs and lows as vividly as then. I have never laughed as much and felt the pit of despair as deeply as then. I suppose I have lived a more muted life, as do most people.

The change from adolescence to adulthood is just as subtle, and it also creeps up on you. Things that previously were exciting and scary became commonplace everyday occurrences. Life just becomes life! It is little wonder that in the autumn of my years I yearn for the colours of my spring and summer days. I find myself trawling through my mind and old photographs and grasping at shadows. Seeking solace from my memories.

Early 70s – Dressed to Kill

In the late sixties the fashion of the day could be described as 'adventurous'. This also carried on into the 70s and the Glam Rock era. I was always a tall lad and, when I was sixteen, I was a thin, gangly youth and had reached six feet tall. What mental illness possessed me to buy a four inch thick pair of platform shoes has been a mystery to me ever since.

I cut a comedic figure as I wobbled along on my 'platforms' like something from a Dick Emery sketch. My flared jeans I didn't consider were flared enough, so Mam had sewn wedges in the sides of them to make them bigger. I added the hippie coat, flowered shirt and long hair to the ensemble and I had completed the image of an absolute idiot.

I used to catch the bus to work dressed like this. Seriously – I really did. I wasn't on my own either. All my mates were dressed in similar hideous ensembles and we would change into our overalls when we got to work. The old chaps on my section took to calling me Deirdre and asking me if I was going for a perm at the weekend. Little did they realise that I was actually considering it!

I loved my platform shoes. They cost me a fortune. They had three different colours of leather in them that ran in stripes over the toe. They were my pride and joy and I wore them to go just about everywhere. There are some pictures of me (unless I have burned them) at a cousin's wedding in a grey suit and my platform shoes. I stood head and shoulders above the rest. It wasn't a good look. Mam insisted on standing on the other side of the crowd when the photo was being taken. She had disowned me.

When I danced in them at the wedding reception I looked a bit like Pinocchio who had messed his trousers, and was trying to shake it first down one leg and then the other. I just looked like an example of 'care in the community' that had gone horribly wrong. To add to the evening, I went over on my ankle, and it was a long way down from those shoes. I hit the ground like a felled tree. I hobbled off the dance floor in total embarrassment.

Some days later I happened to be returning from work. We were all upstairs on the bus, some seven or so of us. Some of the lads smoked so we all congregated up there. The stairs were at the back of the bus and they curved round gracefully until they ended up level with the platform at the back. It was my stop and I clumped my way down the stairs whilst hanging on dearly to the chrome pole that ran vertically down the side of the stairs.

I was about three steps from the bottom and the bus suddenly lurched. I totally lost my footing, and, still clinging tightly to the pole, I swung round it like Johnny Weissmuller in a Tarzan movie and collided with the bus conductress who was standing in the well beside the stairs. I hit her with some force and knocked her leather change bag askew and coins went cascading everywhere. She was livid. She called me a big, gormless, lanky streak of piss and told me to get off her bus. I didn't need asking twice! My mates had witnessed the whole débâcle and were helpless with laughter.

A little later, grey RAF trench coats became fashionable amongst our little clique and we all paraded off to the Army Surplus stores to buy them. Because I was so thin and tall the old boys at work started calling me 'Prisoner of war'. One old chap wasn't happy at all as he was ex RAF himself and saw it as an affront. He would mumble, 'You big Jessie' under his breath whenever I walked past him.

I think things totally came to a head with the old chaps when I rolled in one day sporting a tight, curly perm and wearing round sunglasses. They couldn't do their jobs properly. Every time they looked at me they dissolved into laughter again. One of them said 'He looks like a burnt match.' One remarked on my round sunglasses and asked if they came with a white stick and a Labrador dog. It came as no surprise when I returned after lunch to find a white, freshly painted piece of dowelling around three feet long. All the old sods would say things behind my back, like 'Woof, woof, down boy. Dave control this guide dog of yours.' Oh how I laughed (not really).

Do you know, I don't regret a minute of any of my fashion faux pas. I would hate to have been 'normal' – whatever that is. They were exciting days and the contrast against the garb of the older generation had never been greater than it was then. They say that Rock 'n Roll has come of age and has been accepted as a high art form in its own right. With Band Aid, that music saved an entire nation. Rock 'n Roll hasn't only come of age, it is drawing its pension!

I suppose they said of our generation it was 'sex, drugs and rock n roll'. I didn't get any of the first two. Nowadays it is 'memories, medication and folk music'.

1962 – Over The Wall

I remember the playground in the junior school. It was covered in concrete paving slabs that were most unforgiving if you fell over whilst running. I chipped one of my front teeth doing just that! It also gave me a bleeding and raw chin. One of the teachers put some Dettol into some water, dipped a cotton wool ball into it and unceremoniously slapped this on to my chin.

Had I been in possession of some of the more vulgar and profane swear words, I would certainly have used them. Didn't she realise how much it would sting? She probably did. It was probably revenge for disturbing her tea break! All I did was scream out and she told me not to be a big softie. I wish I had been present when she was in childbirth. I would have loved to have returned the compliment!

I suppose that nowadays a full accident report would have to be filled out. All that happened to me was that I had a bit of gauze stuck on my chin with sticking plaster. When I arrived home, all Mam said was, 'What have you been up to now?' I walked around for two days looking like I had a badly applied false beard! I now also sported a comical smile with my chipped tooth.

Girls in those days still wore pretty cotton dresses and cardigans. Boys wore shirts and jumpers. We all played in the same school playground – but not together. Girls did yucky girls' stuff and boys did manly things like playing football. Girls could entertain themselves with an old washing line that they used as a long skipping rope. There would be a girl at each end of the rope which was whirled round and round, and girls would jump in and out of it and skip. A skill we secretly admired. All the time they were skipping they were chanting bits of rhyming nonsense. Something about monkeys chewing tobacco and rubber dollies – most bizarre!

Along one side of the playground were the girls' and boys' toilets. I'm not sure what the girls toilets looked like, but ours were a row of toilet cubicles and a urinal. The toilet cubicles were enclosed and had roofs, but the urinal was along the wall and open to the elements. At the other side of this wall was the playground. The wall was probably a good eight feet high.

We devised a game called, 'Who can pee the highest?'. We actually left chalk marks on the wall to record our achievements. One lad called Neil became both an instant champion and a legend all in one. He had some kind of technique where he squeezed the end so that a fine but powerful jet of urine was expelled. He pee'd straight over the wall. We then heard a girl on the other side of the wall say, 'I think it's raining.'

Another girl said, 'It's coming from over the wall.' – Then they all ran off screaming to tell teacher. When the teacher arrived on the scene we said that it was a water pistol. When she asked us to produce said water pistol and we didn't, she said, 'I thought not.'

We had to take letters home that read something like, 'Your child has been engaging in unsanitary activities.' Mam was most displeased and asked me what they meant by 'unsanitary activities'. When I told her she just rolled her eyes and sighed. Mam then told Dad. He thought it was hilarious and said, 'God almighty, a bit of piss never harmed nobody.' Mam chided Dad over this and he had to adopt a sombre demeanour, but laughing eyes never lie!

The playground also had a target painted on one wall. The reason why still escapes me to this day. We would use it to kick a football against and add up the scores for an outer, an inner and a bullseye. We would take five shots each from a distance of around ten yards. I often missed the target entirely. The game began to become too simple for some of the lads and they started using a tennis ball instead. It proved too difficult for me.

Girls would also play a game they called 'Two Ball' against the same wall. This involved bouncing first one tennis ball against the wall, closely followed by the second. Whilst one ball was being caught the other was in the air. They also chanted the monkey and rubber doll song to this as well. It became irritating after a while. They also sang another. Something about some ship or other sailing through 'The Ally Ally O'. Were girls a bit retarded, we wondered?

At the end of playtime the teacher rang a big hand bell and we all lined up in two straight rows of boys and girls. We then marched inside in military fashion. We marched down the corridor and across the polished parquet flooring. The wood glowed through a century of polishing over the ages. It glowed with the colour of glossy butterscotch and toffee, and it always had a faint smell of Lavender Polish. We marched on to our classrooms, and lessons would begin. The school yard would fall silent again. No doubt to the relief of the surrounding houses.

1970 First Girlfriend

We met when we were both sixteen and studying for our exams. Up until this time (as they say in these parts) I hadn't been kissed, kicked nor trampled upon. Her name was June. This particular day we were on a field trip to the Yorkshire Dales. We lived a couple of streets apart and the teachers were taking us on the trip in their own cars. With living so close together (a couple of streets apart), we were both picked up by our Geography teacher and his wife and we occupied the back seat of his Mini together for the trip. Our teacher must have only been about 7 or 8 years older than us at the time.

The memory of that trip is clear in my mind. I was shy and a little bit dorky. My parents were poor, so my clothes were never spot on fashion-wise. June, on the other hand, was smartly dressed, and blessed with the looks that required no make-up. She was, in fact, stunning. If she knew the fact that she was so beautiful, she never made a point of showing it. The conversation would have been non-existent if it hadn't been for the teacher's wife periodically speaking to us both over her shoulder.

The field trip was singularly dreary. It involved us trudging over the moorland looking at rock formations. We ended up at a small café at the end of the trip. Next door was a newsagent, so I popped in for a magazine to bury my head in for the journey home. I picked up a weighty magazine called *The Dalesman* – that should occupy me for a couple of hours, I thought!

We loaded ourselves on to the back seat of the mini again for the cringe-worthy journey home and I pulled out the magazine from my pocket and started reading – well when I say reading, all I was doing was looking idly at words and trying to stay awake. After a few minutes, she leaned slightly towards me, which instantly made me alert and awake. She seemed to be interested in reading the book I had. I turned to look at her and she gave me the softest of smiles and said, 'Can we share?' After seeing the look on my face (I must have looked like a rabbit in someone's headlights) she said, 'the book – can we read it together?' I said 'yeah, no problem'.

I held one side of the book and she held the other. The publication in question was no bigger than *The Readers Digest*, so we got quite cozy on the back seat. Occasionally, when we hit a bend on the tight country lanes she would slide further towards me and I could feel the warmth of her soft body against mine, and smell whatever perfumed item she was wearing. It was a heady mixture – the journey home just flew by.

A couple of days later, her best friend approached me and asked me what I thought about June, and did I like her. I answered that yes I liked her and that she was always nice to me. She then said, 'No Dave, I mean do you LIKE her?' I asked her if she meant 'like' in a sort of girlfriend/boyfriend way. She said yes – she meant exactly that. I just broke out into a nervous laugh and said, 'But she's gorgeous!' She said that yes, she agreed she was gorgeous, and for some odd reason, also interested in me!! The day after I made a point of walking home with June to try and pluck up the courage to ask her out. I was so insecure I still wondered if I was the target of some cruel joke. I had practised all these cool speeches in my mind. In the end we were just feet away from her garden gate when I just blurted out 'Would you, er, kind of, er, well, sort of...erm, go out with me?' She said OK. I hadn't thought this far along the unlikely scenario. She stood patiently before saying, 'well?' I said..'oh yeah...erm thanks.' She rolled her eyes and said, 'Well shall I just wait at the end of the street in case you turn up, or shall we say where and when we will meet'.

The date was made and we went out together for some ten months or so. Never ever have I been so head-over-heels since then. Not only did I put her on a pedestal and worship her, I even worshipped the pedestal I put her on! My love, my life and everything was complete. I wanted for nothing.

The day we broke up is another story. The sick, churning in the pit of my stomach as she said those words, 'Dave, I don't want to see you again'. I could physically feel my legs turning to jelly and my world crumbling around me. Life went on, but I don't think I was ever the same again afterwards.

1968 – My First Pint

It was my younger sister's wedding day. Dad wasn't well enough to walk her down the aisle, so the honour was passed over to my Uncle Bob. My sister looked radiant in her wedding dress. Many of my aunts were weeping and saying things like, 'Ee, doesn't she look lovely?' The vows were spoken and they were hitched, so all went off as planned and we headed off for the reception.

It had always been assumed that Dad would buy me my first pint. It was almost a rite of passage. I would have been introduced to all at his local and he would have shown me off with pride. He would then have bought me my first pint. The old warrior and the young. Two men side by side. Pint in hand. I had played this scenario over and over in my mind. I knew exactly how it would have all happened, but it didn't happen that way.

Dad was at the wedding reception seated in a comfortable chair. He wasn't too good on his legs. My new brother-in-law called me over and he said, 'What are you drinking?' I said, 'I'll have a bitter lemon please.' He said, 'No, what are you DRINKING?'. I wasn't expecting the question, so I just said what I had heard others say. I said, 'I'll have a pint.' He looked at me and said, 'Good choice, what of?' I asked him what they had. He said, 'Well they have bitter, lager, mild...' I stopped him at mild and said, 'I'll have a pint of mild please'. It sounded to me like it would be the gentlest. After all it was called mild, wasn't it?

The pint was pulled and handed to me. I thanked my brother-in-law and was about to put the glass to my lips when I saw my Dad sitting in his chair. I made my excuses and said something like, 'This glass is heavy, I'm sitting down'. I went and sat by Dad.

He saw the pint in my hand. I broke the ice and said, 'Well Dad, our first pint together just like you said – you owe your son-in-law for my pint.

I saw his eyes mist over a little. He understood the situation perfectly. He said to me, 'You're a good lad, do you know that?' and I answered, 'Aye, I do. You tell me often enough.' We both laughed and Dad said, 'Drink yer mild.'

I took a goodly sip out of the glass and it tasted bloody awful. I never flinched at all. I just put down the glass and let out a contented but theatrical sigh, followed by a small burp.

That mild lasted the best part of an hour. My glass was at last thankfully empty. As if by magic another one appeared in front of me. Mam said to me, 'Make that your last one.' I was happy to do just that. It was awful. I slowly sipped my way through a second pint and it was time to go home. I felt strangely warm and happy and the urge to giggle was upon me. Mam linked my arm and my Dad with the other arm and walked us both to the taxi. As soon as the fresh air hit me the booze kicked in a little more. We drove off in the taxi and the drowsiness took over. The last thing I remember is Mam laughing and saying something about, 'One sniff of the barmaid's apron.'

When we arrived home, Mam gently woke me and helped me out of the taxi. All I wanted to do was go to bed. I felt shattered. I would have gone to bed in my suit if she would have let me – shoes and all. Mam made me get into my pyjamas and insisted I had a cup of tea before I went to bed. I sipped my hot tea gratefully. Mam always knew best.

Dad smiled at me. I think he was remembering earlier in the

evening and my first pint. He gave me a warm smile and a wink and I smiled back. It had been one of those milestone moments, not quite as planned but a milestone nonetheless. I'm glad I didn't just take a drink when it was offered to me but brought it back to sit beside Dad. It was as if someone had tapped me on the shoulder and pointed the way. Thank God my guardian angel had done his job!

1961 – Having My Tonsils Out

After several sore throats and visits to the doctors for tonsillitis and other throat infections, it was decided that my tonsils needed to come out. Being so young (I was still five years old) this was kept from me until the very day I had to go into hospital.

This story is assembled from the loose threads and coloured ribbons that dwell in my mind. There may be some inaccuracies, but this is how I remember it.

My mother, my eldest sister and myself alighted from the bus outside the Hospital. An old, converted Manor House with a scattering of modern buildings surrounding it. We spent a few minutes beside an ornamental pond with ducks and coots bobbing along merrily on it. I still had no idea what was happening at this time.

Mam then knelt down in front of me so that she could look directly into my eyes. She then told me that I had to be a big, brave soldier and that they were leaving me here to have my tonsils out. 'Leaving me here?' I thought to myself. Will it be like school? Will Mam pick me up tonight? All these questions were tumbling round inside my head. My cosy little five-year-old world was coming apart at the seams. The world had been turned upside down, and with it – my stomach.

They walked me to the appointed ward. As we were walking along, my sister said to my mum, 'Awwww bless him, he is shaking like a leaf.' I remember that my teeth were actually chattering with sheer fear. I was shown to a little cubicle with two beds in it. A boy of a similar age to me was already occupying the other bed. Mam and my sister said their goodbyes and I immediately burst into tears – this in turn triggered off the other lad into a similar bawling episode. I was later told that Mam wasn't in a much better state after she left the ward.

A round faced, jolly nurse came in and told us it would all be fine and not to cry, and after it was all over we were allowed to have bowlfuls of lovely ice cream to soothe our throats. She handed out some crayons and a colouring book to each of us and soon we were happily playing together. He told me his name was Geoffrey.

We were scheduled for surgery the day afterwards. We were talking together after lights out and he asked me, 'Are you scared like me?' I told him that I was. We both cried ourselves to sleep.

I awoke the following morning to find that Geoffrey had already gone. A while later he was wheeled back into our little room. He was still fast asleep in his bed. I was told to leave him to 'have a little sleep'. The next thing my bed was also being wheeled out of the room. I was ushered into theatre and they lifted me onto what I thought was another bed. It must have been the operating table.

Beside me was a machine that had four glass tubes on it. Each glass tube was filled with a different coloured liquid. One a kingfisher blue like the colour of an ice pop. Another was bright yellow, and the other colours I can't remember. It was made of shiny chrome and had tubes and switches all over it. Now, I have to admit that I THINK I saw this. After discussing this with nurses from that era in more recent days, none of them had any idea what I was talking about. They say I may have been delirious with the anaesthetic – anything is possible I suppose! Very shortly afterwards a mask was placed over my face and they told me to breathe in. I was soon out like a light.

Some time later I awoke to the feeling that someone had force-fed me barbed wire. I croaked for the nurse and she came over to me and said, 'How are we feeling my lovely?' and she tried to sit me up and place a pillow behind me. I promptly threw up all over the front of her lovely, starched uniform. Expecting to be told off, I burst out crying. She said, 'It's okay sweetheart,' and gave me a hug. It must have happened regularly to her. Even so, she was wonderful about it. She gave me a kiss on my forehead and told me to get some sleep.

I awoke refreshed some time later and asked the nurse where my big bowl of ice cream was. She chuckled and told me that I had to eat something 'proper' first. She presented me with a bowl of cornflakes with precious little milk on them and a spoon and I was told to eat up. It was horrendous. It was like trying to swallow broken glass. I got through about half of it and the nurse told me I had done very well and to have another little nap. When I awoke the nurse was smiling down on me. She said 'Are you ready for that ice cream now?' My face said it all. She laughed and plonked down a bowlful of Neapolitan Ice Cream in front of me. She told me to eat it slowly or I would make myself sick.

A little later Mam and my sister showed up and brought me toys and books. Geoffrey and I played with them.

I can't remember when Mam collected me. It may have been the day after. I was told I was in for another treat. A big, black Taxi was waiting outside to take us home. Out of all the trauma and fear I had emerged back into a wonderful, loving world where I felt safe. When I thought back about it all, in later years, it brought it home to me. Kids don't need 'things' they need love and security. The latest gadget will never replace the time you spend with your kids.

Soon I was home and in my pyjamas. Dad had brought my bed downstairs so I could sit up in the front room and watch telly. The last memory of all this was Mam buying me this wonderful drink. It was a bottle that was wrapped in yellow coloured cellophane. I was told it was called Lucozade. To this day I still can't pass it on a shelf in a shop without being reminded of having my tonsils out.

Late 60s – The Dark Art of Snogging

Around the age of fourteen, as did most boys of my age, I began to view girls in a whole new light. To us boys, the girls of our age seemed to be like mini adults. They certainly started to develop a more interesting shape for a start, and were far more mature and wily than we were.

Girls would usually meander around in groups, sitting on a wall or around a table in school, making them virtually unapproachable by a single boy (with a few confident exceptions). The exceptions were the good-looking, athletic types who were on the football or rugby team. These were often a bit more muscular than us. They used to turn the girls into simpering, giggling, doe-eyed little bunny rabbits, hopping around at their feet – we hated them!

The girls would hold conversations amongst themselves. Occasionally one would turn and stare at a passing boy and they would all break into giggles, which usually resulted in the boy blushing and making a hurried exit. We were like a group of timid wildebeest being looked down upon with semi-amusement by a pride of lionesses who had just recently devoured one of our kind and were no longer hungry – probably not far from the truth!

We boys would brag that we had snogged loads of girls. We would point at a girl and say 'Snogged that'. Usually we were lying. No, we were ALWAYS lying!

Girls seemed to be blessed with a natural skill and aptitude for kissing. Where on earth did they learn this? My first introduction to this was at one class Christmas party. We had decided to play 'spin the bottle' and when my turn came I got to kiss a delightful, kind and pretty girl called Joyce. She planted a real good one on me. It was breathtaking (quite literally). I tingled all over and bits of me began to stir. After the kiss she just gave me a coy little innocent smile, knowing full well she had left a dumb-struck, grinning wreck of a boy behind in her wake. I had to be told to sit back down in the circle as I just stood and watched in a trance as she walked away.

I remarked later to my friend that she had been a little careless and had accidentally let her tongue stray into my mouth and touch my tongue. He looked at me with a wearied expression for a second or two before saying, 'Dave, we need to talk.'

For some reason, at that age we believed that performing stupid stunts in front of them would make us look more desirable. It never worked, but it did provide them with some amusement at our expense when we came a cropper, as happened to me once when I tried to ride my bike past them without holding on to the handlebars. The gravel rash on my chin made me look most attractive indeed!

These were painfully embarrassing days. I still cringe when I think back at what a buffoon I must have been. The one comforting thought is that I was far from alone or unique in feeling this way. I had seen some spectacular stunts and dares go publicly and hilariously wrong, leaving the poor beggar on the end of it as a sort of school legend as the story got told and re-told about his downfall.

That which does not kill us makes us stronger – maybe so. It can also leave you with a memory bank filled with cringe-worthy tales. Girls eh?

1960s – Recycling and Dubious Literature

When late October arrived, and the nights grew dark and colder, our minds would drift towards the idea of building a bonfire. The first thing we would do would be to pick a place. This was usually the patch of spare ground alongside the houses. We would then collect any bits of wood that were lying around in the immediate vicinity. After that we would start knocking on doors. 'Have you got anything for our bommie?' we would ask. Usually there would be some surplus bits and pieces hanging around. We would usually end up with at least one threadbare sofa. We were actually providing quite a useful service to these people when I think about it.

We loved sofas and armchairs as we would ferret down the back of them and find the odd coin. You would hear such cries as, 'Look, a threepenny bit'. All proceeds were shared out equally amongst ourselves. If it was only a solitary threepenny bit, we would buy sweets and share these out instead. We would occasionally find a half crown or a florin. This would be like discovering a Roman coin hoard to us. We would find all kinds of things down the back of the sofas. Old bits of disgusting food detritus, the odd toy soldier, we once found an intact condom in its little packet.

We were also given other stuff to dispose of. Old carpets and rugs, the occasional Piano, sideboards, all kinds of things. We knocked on one door and were given a pile of old newspapers. Tucked between the newspapers we found a small box. When we opened the box we found a hypodermic syringe, complete with a needle, and a couple of ampoules of liquid. We took it back to the house from whence it came. It was received with utmost gratitude. We were given a shilling for our trouble. I have no idea what the contents of the little glass ampoules contained.

We knocked on one door and a man opened the door and we asked if he had anything for the bonfire. He said, 'Wait there'. A moment later he came back with a cardboard box. He looked around in a strange manner, as if checking to see if anyone was looking, before handing the box to us. We thanked him and left.

We had a little den in the middle of the bonfire. We took the box inside the den to look at the contents. There were about fifty copies of a certain gentlemen's magazine by the name of *Parade*. These contained pictures of scantily clad ladies and stories of a lurid nature. The odd copy was later stashed inside our school duffel bags as an example of our secret library. Other kids paid us in sweets to borrow them. We had quite a little lucrative business going!

One day it came to the attention of older boys at school that we had a pornographic lending library. They threatened us with physical violence if we didn't tell them where we kept the magazines. They took the magazines off us and took them away. Revenge was served upon them sometime later as one of them was caught reading one of them in class. All the other boys were also rounded up after a search of their school bags. They got the cane and a letter was sent out to their parents. Imagine their parents' reaction when they received a letter informing them that their son had been found in possession of adult literature. No doubt they got another clout at home too.

When I think of all the wonderful pieces of old furniture that found their way onto the bonfire after they had been replaced by some hideous, Formica topped piece of garbage. Well I could almost weep. I do, however, remember one man approaching us at our bonfire and saying 'I'll give you two bob for that cupboard'. We readily agreed and he carefully carried it away and placed it in the back of a van. He looked through the rest of the bonfire and found nothing else that took his fancy, and he drove away. I often wonder what we gave away for a couple of bob, and what it would be worth today!

When the glorious fifth of November arrived, the bonfire would be lit, and all the neighbours would bring out treats like Parkin (a type of ginger cake) and treacle toffee which were distributed amongst everyone. The fireworks would be lit, and a good time was had by all. When the bonfire had died down, potatoes would be placed amongst the glowing embers to cook. They would be fished out later with a stick and left to cool a little before the blackened outer crust was scraped away and the potato was broken open and eaten with a spoon. The outside would be fluffy and delicious, but there was always a raw chunk of potato left in the middle. It was a fine art timing it just right.

By morning, all that would be left of the bonfire were the odd unburned bits of timber and bits of metal. We would collect the hinges to be used on such things as home made fishing tackle boxes. The old nails and screws would be left to puncture someone's bicycle tyre at a later date.

1963 – Casualty

I was always in some scrape or other as a kid, and a couple of these scrapes ended up with a visit to the local infirmary casualty department. There weren't the long waiting times that we seem to have these days. I think people didn't like to be seen to be wasting the time of the doctors and nurses – so it had to be for something that needed fairly immediate treatment. The infirmary was around three miles away from home, so it was a bus ride or a lift from someone.

On one particular day I had been out fishing and had been bitten by a horsefly near my thumb. It made my hand look like a rubber glove that someone had partially inflated. Mam kept a close eye on it, but when she noticed a red line that was developing and beginning to run up my wrist, she whisked me off to hospital. When we arrived, she spoke to reception and we were shown straight into an examination cubicle. The Doctor examined my hand and asked the nurse to give me a tetanus injection. He also requested an antibiotic shot (or I believe that is what it was). Both were injected into my backside – which I was glad about. I was a little bit squeamish about needles!

The Doctor discussed my case with my mother. He spoke about leaving me in all night for observation. She must have seen the look of panic on my face. She promised him that she would watch me closely, and phone an ambulance if I took a turn for the worse. This alarmed me even further – an AMBULANCE?? Just how bad *was* this?

We arrived back home and a bed was made for me on the couch so that Mam could keep an eye on me. This was a minor inconvenience as my two sisters had nowhere to sit, but they didn't mind sitting on the rug to watch TV. Mam checked my wrist every half hour or so and put her hand on my forehead to check my temperature. After a couple of hours, the red line began to fade, and so it was deemed safe for me to go to bed. In the morning, my hand had reduced drastically in size, and the red line had gone entirely.

The other notable visit occurred when a couple of friends and I were out on our bikes on a summer's day. I had worn glasses since being around six years old. I wore them all the time – they never came off apart from bedtime and bathing, etc. This particular day, we were riding along when somehow a wasp had managed to fly against my face and get trapped behind my glasses. It stung me three times in all, just beneath my eyebrow. The pain was excruciating. I pedalled like fury for home. My friends later told me that I was uncatchable. They had never seen anyone pedal so fast.

My eyelid swelled up like a ping-pong ball and I looked a mess. Mam was mildly panicked. She knocked on a neighbour's door to ask if he would run us to hospital. When he saw my eye, he didn't need asking twice. We sped through the streets and arrived at casualty minutes later. He let Mam and me out and went to park up and wait for us.

As before, I was shown almost immediately into a cubicle and examined. The doctor examined my eye. He forced open the eyelids which made me scream out in pain. He informed us that my eye, although red, looked fine. Again I received the ubiquitous tetanus injection in the backside. At this rate I would be immune to just about everything, I thought to myself. He said that the eye looked alarming, but the swelling would soon go down. He put something onto a lint pad and applied this to my eye, holding it in place with surgical tape. It felt very soothing. He said to Mam to take it off in the morning and come back in if it was no different, or had become worse.

I am pleased to report that much of the swelling had gone down the day after. Mam replaced the lint pad over my eye, but in the absence of surgical tape, she used bits of sticking plaster. When I put my glasses back on over the top of this arrangement I must have looked a comical sight!

Late 1960s – The Night We Almost Frightened Tony to Death

Tony was a happy-go-lucky sort of boy. He was part of our particular group. We would all 'look out' for him when we were out there in the big, bad world, as he was a little younger than the rest of us. One day we decided we would have a bit of a giggle at Tony's expense. We had pre-arranged all the parts that everyone was to play in advance. Even as we were planning it, we were already laughing.

It was November, and it was dark by six o'clock. It would be around seven in the evening. Mam was out at her friend's and we had the house to ourselves. I had previously rigged up the house by tying bits of fishing line to certain objects. We were all sitting around playing on the coffee table with a sort of improvised Ouija Board. It was a glass on a smooth topped coffee table with the alphabet written on separate bits of paper, and the words 'yes' and 'no' arranged in a circle around it. We played with this for a while. We pushed the glass around to spell out dire messages and warnings. This had the effect of making Tony more than a little nervous.

I then went on to say, 'Lets have a séance.' I went on to ask in my most melodramatic voice, 'Is there anybody there? – give us a sign.' One of the lads pulled on a bit of fishing line and a toasting fork flew off the wall.

Tony let out a bit of a yelp and said, 'I want to go home.' We all told him not to be silly, as we were here to protect him. We pulled onto the floor other assorted ornaments with other bits of fishing line and Tony was definitely in a state of severe agitation.

It was at this time that Bernard announced that he had to be home as his Mam was going out. This had been pre-arranged. He wasn't going home at all, but made his way upstairs to Mam's room to hide in the built-in wardrobe as arranged.

A little later, I suggested that it would be a great idea if we turned off all the lights and all played hide-and-seek in the dark. Tony didn't seem at all keen. I said, 'It's fine – stick with me.'

Geoff had been designated as the seeker and we all ran off to hide. I told Tony to stick by me. We ran upstairs and I told him that I was going to hide under the bed. I told Tony to get into the built-in wardrobe (where we had previously planted Bernard). Tony got into the wardrobe just as we intended. After thirty seconds or so, Bernard issued forth an eerie wail and reached out to touch Tony on his shoulder whilst saying, 'GOT YOU!'

The built-in wardrobe doors sprang open like a haunted cuckoo-clock, closely followed by the rapidly exiting Tony. I had never heard a boy scream like a girl before! I saw him clear the bed I was lying underneath by a considerable distance. I then saw him hit the bedroom floor as he continued to scream loudly. He headed for the stairs. He hit the stairs landing by totally bypassing the three steps that led down to it. There he fell into a heap, still screaming wildly.

When we turned on the lights, he was still in shock. One of the lads said, 'He is a funny colour and his lips are blue.' We all agreed that perhaps we had overdone it all a bit! Tony went home.

His Mam played merry hell with us all a day later. She told us that he now insisted sleeping with the light on. We all looked solemnly at his Mam as she told us this, but inside we were already chalking ourselves up as legends. A cruel prank, and one I am not at all proud of – but it was funny at the time.

Some days later I was asleep in my bed. I used to sleep on my stomach. I was awoken by the distinct feeling of someone of some weight sitting on my feet. Fully expecting it to be my sister I kicked out and felt my foot hit against a body. I flew around in bed whilst shouting, 'Sod off!' expecting to see my sister, but the room was empty and the door still closed. No one could have exited the room that quickly and shut the door behind themselves. I switched on the bedside lamp just in time to see the window curtains swaying. I thought the wind had been blowing them until I realised that the window was closed.

Just then, and for no reason, a book fell off my bedside table. It is fair to say that I was now totally awake. It was daylight before I dared drift off to sleep. Maybe it was a case of the ghosts getting their revenge for the prank. I slept with the lights on too that night.

1962 – The Party When Mam Got Drunk

It was the New Year's Eve party of 1962. We decided we would hold a small 'do' in our front room. Mam had been baking all day and had also made dozens of sandwiches. Dad had bought three or four crates of beer and a little something for the ladies – this consisted of a dozen bottles each of Cherry B and Babycham. A group of some twenty or so relatives, neighbours and friends had been invited.

People started to arrive around 8pm and Dad was seated at the piano. After a couple of drinks the crowd became loosened up and soon song requests were coming thick and fast at Dad. An old lady said, 'Sing *Nobody's Child*.' Dad obliged and soon all the ladies were having an emotional moment. They were all blubbing whilst singing the line '*No mommy's kisses and no daddy's smiles, nobody loves me, I'm nobody's child.*' Dad said, 'OK this is getting a bit maudlin,' and launched into *Roll Out The Barrel*.

Soon after, the floor was given over to the record player and the strains of '*Let's Twist Again*' filled the room and a few of the more mature people gave their own unique attempt at the twist whilst the younger ones rolled their eyes.

I had been allowed special dispensation to stay up until after the chimes at midnight. By 10pm I was feeling the strain so went into the kitchen and curled myself up on a chair and had a nap. At approximately 11pm I was rudely awakened by someone playing a trumpet of some kind. Let's just say that they were either still learning the instrument or in no fit state of sobriety to be playing it.

The crowd thought it hilarious and loudly jeered at every bum note played.

I went into the front room; the party was buzzing and Mam was sitting on the sofa with a sort of melancholic look on her face. I asked Dad if Mam was okay. He said, 'Probably not, son – she has had six Cherry B's and a Babycham.' I asked him if that was a lot. He said, 'It is for your Mam!'

He then went on to tell me that Mam got 'a bit touchy' when she had a drink or two. He told me that he had already had the 'Do you love me, do you Seth, tell me?' and the tears when Dad said, 'Of course I do luv,' and Mam answered, 'No you don't, waaaaaaaa.' Now apparently Mam was just sliding towards her, 'Don't touch me and don't speak to me, you bastard.' stage. Dad had seen this before. When I asked him if he was going to go and talk to Mam, he said, 'No bloody fear – she will kick off.'

Midnight approached and soon everyone made a big circle in the middle of the living room floor and were singing *Auld Lang Syne* – including Mam who seemed to be laughing at just about everything and having a little bit of trouble controlling her legs. Ten minutes later the party settled down to quieter music and Mam was being counselled by a couple of her friends, saying such things as, 'They are all bastards, Mary,' and 'You were always too good for him.'

As 1 a.m approached, everyone left the house to cheery (and beery) goodbyes. It was time to go to bed. Dad told my sister to take the bucket upstairs in case 'Mam wasn't well'. Then came something like a comedy sketch as we tried to get Mam upstairs. It was like a Chuckle Brothers show. Back a bit. To me. To you. Eventually, and after a few close calls, Mam was led to the bedroom and left to the care of Dad.

The day after, Mam had an upset stomach. She told Dad that perhaps it was one of those ham sandwiches that had been on the turn.

Dad gave a sardonic chuckle and said, 'Happen you are right luv, that would be it.' It was one of those convenient lies that were supposed to protect me from the truth that occasionally, grown-ups acted a bit daft.

At lunch Dad asked Mam if she wanted a Cherry B with her lunch. She seemed to grow a little pale and said, 'I'll pass thanks.' Dad smiled and poured out a Guinness in front of her before quaffing half the glass and saying, 'Ahhhhhh, lovely.'

Mam called him an animal and we all ate our dinner in peace and quiet.

1960s – Mrs Jackson

At the far end of our street was where Mrs Jackson lived. You could tell that at one time her house had been a shop. There was a long glass window that had once been the shop front. This was now adorned with a net curtain that covered the lower half of the window. Everyone referred to these net curtain arrangements as a 'Balance'. It was to afford the occupant a little privacy from prying eyes as they walked past her window. At night, she had heavy tapestry style curtains that she would draw across to block out the world.

The older ones knew Mrs Jackson when the shop was actually a shop. It had been a milliner's and also sold wool for knitting and other bits and pieces. Oddly enough she had also sold paraffin from a shed arrangement in the back yard! The shop had closed its doors to trade in 1950 before I was born. I have to admit that she scared us a little as kids.

Mrs Jackson was from another world and not really from our neck of the woods at all. The story goes that her parents had been church people who had been born and bred in rural Cheshire, and at one time had been missionaries out in India. Perhaps she viewed selling hats to the ladies of my small mining town as missionary work – who knows?

On rare occasions – perhaps when she took down her net curtains to clean them, we would get a glimpse inside her front room (or parlour as she knew it). It was like peering in through the window of one of those Victorian museums where they have left a room as it was from the turn of the century. She had an old, upright piano which still had the candlesticks on it, resplendent with actual candles in them. On top of this were a pair of silver photo frames with old sepiatone photographs in them. The one thing that really gave us kids the creeps was a large stuffed owl that sat under a glass dome on a small occasional table.

I think it was this owl that first led us into believing that she was a witch. One of the older boys told us that one night she had left a gap in the curtains and he peeped through to see her lift the glass dome from off the owl and he had seen it come to life!! This shook us to the core. We also believed she could cast spells and curses. I think Mrs Jackson knew this, but it suited her purpose as it kept us away from her property and from under her feet.

The theory was further compounded by the way she dressed. All the women in our street wore headscarves, but Mrs Jackson wore a hat. Probably a creation of her own making from her time in the millinery trade. Her clothes had once been smart and probably fashionable back in the early 40s but now looked a little tired. In truth she was just a refined old lady getting along with life. Any of the men who passed her would doff their caps and say things like, 'How are you this morning, Mrs Jackson?' She would exchange pleasantries and drift on by.

Mam informed me one day that she wanted me to help one of the neighbours with a few jobs she wanted doing. Imagine my shock when she said it was Mrs Jackson. She had seen my eyes widen with fear and she laughed and said, 'She's a funny old stick but she doesn't bite. You will be fine'. I wasn't at all sure! I arrived at the door of Mrs Jackson and timidly knocked.

Mrs Jackson opened the door. She looked me up and down and, without smiling, she said, 'David, isn't it? I nodded back at her. She said, 'Well come on in, and don't touch anything unless I give you

111

permission.' She took me through the parlour where her 'familiar' the stuffed owl lay asleep under his glass dome, through her kitchen and into the back yard. In a corner of the yard lay the little lean-to shed that had probably housed the paraffin store.

All that remained of it now was a pile of old and rotting wood. She gave me a claw hammer, a saw and an axe and left me with instructions to pull out all the rusty old nails from the planks of wood and put them in a cardboard box to be thrown away. I was then to saw up the wood and chop it to make firewood. It was my kind of job; playing around with tools and sawing stuff up. A little later I got careless. The saw slipped and gouged a little chunk out of my knuckle. It was just a graze but it bled profusely. I timidly shouted inside for Mrs Jackson.

She said, 'Whatever is the matter?' I held up my bleeding knuckle, and with a pout I said, 'I've gone and cut myself.' She guided me into the kitchen where she took a clean, damp cloth and gently dabbed my knuckle, then she dried it and wrapped a piece of cloth around it and tied it. She smiled at me and said, 'You are a brave little thing, aren't you?'

I didn't know what to say, so I said nothing. She then went on to say, 'Especially as you have come to the house of the big, bad witch,' and then she laughed.

My eyes were now the size of saucers. She said, 'It's time for a cup of tea and some toast, and bade me to sit at her table in the kitchen. She then started telling me stories of when she had lived in India and how her Dad was very strict but also kind. She told me about seeing elephants and tigers and all about the games she would play with the servants' children in the grounds of their house.

After an hour or so of sipping our tea and eating our toast she said, 'You have done a lot of work out there, there is quite a pile of wood. Would you like to come back tomorrow and do some more?' I eagerly nodded my head and then she gave me a warm hug and pressed a shilling into the palm of my hand. So, all the press about her had been wrong. I also never saw the stuffed owl move either.

Word had got around our little gang of kids that I had been inside the witch's house. When I said that it was all rubbish and that she was nice, one lad said, 'No she isn't. She has cast a spell on you. She is wicked.' I asked him to take it back but he refused and just laughed at me, so I lamped him one and sent him sprawling across the floor. I leant over him and said, 'Don't you call her names.'

I didn't really care what they thought. In fact, I was secretly glad in many ways. She was my own, private little secret friend. I didn't want to share her with these ruffians, I thought. (Ruffians eh? – when I think back I think a few of her manners had started rubbing off on me!) The work took me a couple more visits and she topped the overall money up by another one and sixpence to half a crown. Each day we had tea and toast and each day we chatted about India and her life before opening the shop. Mam was right – she was indeed a funny old stick, but also a kind one.

Early 60s – My Shoe Cleaning Business

I remember my Dad showing me how to clean and polish a pair of his shoes. He told me about putting the polish onto the end of a cloth and then rubbing it into the shoe leather with a circular motion. I was then to take a brush and buff it until the polish began to gleam and that I was to spit onto the shoe as it increased the shine. I was then shown how to buff the shoe to a final polish with a soft cloth.

Dad left me with all his shoes and came back some twenty minutes later. All his shoes were paired up and put together all in a neat row. He examined them and told me I had done a wonderful job. He fumbled in his pocket and brought out some change. He then handed me a nice, shiny sixpence. I was absolutely made up.

This got me to thinking. There's money in this shoe cleaning lark! I asked Mam if I could borrow the shoe cleaning box as I was off to make my fortune. She laughed and said, 'Go for it.' My first job was Mr Roberts next door. I knocked on his door and told him what a good shoe cleaner I was and that Dad said how great his shoes looked.

He said OK and invited me in. He dropped two pairs of shoes in front of me and said, 'Let's see how you get on.'

He came back a few minutes later to check on my progress. I had already done one pair of shoes and was finishing the second pair. He picked up the first pair of shoes and said, 'Wow, these are really shiny – well done.'

114

As this was my first commercial job I was eager to do good work, so I decided to polish the soles as well. I soon found that I couldn't get all the polish from between the ridges. I thought to myself, well no one is going to see it, and just left it. He thanked me and gave me threepence.

I knocked on around ten doors and polished countless shoes. I had made about three and sixpence by the end of the day. I had people saying such things to me as, 'Come again.' and 'I hate cleaning shoes – come again next week.'

The day after the shoe cleaning episode, Dad walked into the kitchen. He was howling with laughter. Mr Roberts from next door had collared Dad and told him about me cleaning his shoes. Dad had asked him if I had done a good job. He said, 'Yes, a bit too good of a job. He also polished the soles and didn't tell me.'

Apparently he had been all ready to go out the night before. He'd donned his gleaming shoes and taken a step onto the lino. As the soles of his shoes met the lino, the polish acted as a perfect lubricant. He told Dad that as he fell he grabbed the tablecloth and pulled the milk jug and sugar bowl all over himself.

It was the end of a promising young career in the service industry. I had been thwarted from making my fortune for doing too good a job! Mam made me go round to all the houses I had visited and inform them of the fact that I had turned their shoes into a potential hazard. They all laughed when I re-told the story about what had happened to poor Mr Roberts. Some said that they had already noticed and not to worry.

Dad polished his own shoes after that!

Believing – Early 60s

As a small child, I used to leave little presents for the fairies at the bottom of the garden. I would leave little pieces of biscuit for them. Of course, when I returned the morning after, these would be gone. It was a thrill for me, and also, to me, the proof of their existence. It never crossed my mind that they had been eaten by birds or mice. A child's mind is blessed with the magic of innocence. To small children anything is possible, and everything WAS possible.

We were able to suspend belief. Even as older children, we would allow fantasy to rule our minds. A stick became anything, from a sword to a rifle. We could invent games around just about anything. An old tin can had several uses. It was a substitute ball for clattering and noisy games of street football. It was a water collecting vessel for making mud pies, it was also a target for throwing stones or a catapult. Punch a hole in the bottom of two cans and thread a piece of string between them and pull the string tight and we had a phone!

We would take off the serrated edged lids from tins and punch two small holes close together with a nail near the centre of the lid. We would thread a length of string through both holes in a loop and tie the loose ends together. When the can lid was rotated it tightened up the string. When pulled, the can lid would whizz round. Centrifugal force would keep the lid spinning around, first one way, and then the other, when the string was repeatedly pulled. We could cut through small twigs with these.

I think children today have partially lost this gift. They are given bright and exciting toys from almost day one that are covered in things to press and twirl around. They are sat in front of a TV set to watch *Peppa Pig* or *In The Night Garden*. All in full and glorious colour. Give them an empty cotton reel to play with, and they will look at you as if you are on medication! If they went to school and told their teachers they were given a stick to play with, or the sharp lid of a baked beans tin, they would probably call the social workers!

Imagination is the most powerful tool possessed by a child's mind, and the loss of innocence, make-believe and whimsy are its biggest enemies. This is why I immerse myself in films of fantasy. I am craving the sweet taste of innocence once again. Try as I might to believe and relive those days, my mind falls a little short, as my present day imaginings are annoyed by 'adult thoughts' such as, Ah this reminds me of a work by Lewis Carroll. or some such unnecessary academic thought. I even tried sitting on the sofa dressed in my pyjamas with a cup of cocoa as in childhood days. All that happened was I thought to myself, This cocoa doesn't taste as nice as it once did, and the cynic inside me had won again.

I suppose, as children, we weren't starved of colour, but often assaulted by it. The garish, bright colours of the sixties left little room for such minor things as subtlety and good taste. Even the once stately cars that were in classic black, maroon or dark green were superseded by pastel shades and bright yellows and blues. Our Formica topped kitchen table was covered in abstract blocks of pale blue, yellow and grey squares. Even the shopping came in day-glo packets with explosively worded slogans. We consumed Ice Pops, which were plastic-wrapped, frozen sticks of garishly coloured liquid which were of colours that didn't naturally occur in nature. We were surrounded by over-stimulation of the worst kind. It is little wonder we craved the natural colours of Mother Nature.

Our senses were as sharp as razor blades and not yet dulled by a wearying and cynical world. Things tasted better. Feelings were experienced with more intensity. We hadn't yet forgotten that life was wondrous and was there to squeeze every drop from. I can't remember the last time I had butterflies in my stomach. Probably the last time I saw a brown envelope marked *Inland Revenue* drop through my letterbox.

They have classes at school in all kinds of things these days, such as Drama and Computer Sciences. Perhaps they should have classes in whimsy and primitive play, where they are told to suspend belief and actually experience the thrill of imagination. Where they are given a builders' plank and asked to build a see-saw by placing it over the top of a pile of bricks. Or are shown how to make a rope swing by tying the rope to the branch of a big, old tree – but of course Health and Safety wouldn't allow it, would they – bless their ever-so-tight little hearts!

My Castle was a pile of bricks
my shield a dustbin lid.
My sword a stick – Excalibur
when I was just a kid.
Imagined realms where dragons played
and Goblins danced with glee.
Where fairy kings they all held court
beneath that old oak tree.
I could be a cowboy bold
or soldier with his gun.
Games were played with no remorse
and everything was fun.
When life today it wearies me
I think of those times mild.
I've learned to throw off all my years
and play just like a child.

D. Hayes 2016

Ben – 1970

At school one of the subjects I always liked was Woodwork. The workshop always had that delightful smell of wood (of course), glue and the smell of the oil and wax used to polish the finished products. Woodwork was such a tactile thing!

Our woodwork teacher was a kind-hearted Yorkshireman by the name of Mr Cooper (or Ben as we all secretly called him); he was somewhere in his 50s. He was always caring and never quick to chastise. He would just say, 'No lad, do it like this,' and then show you. When the penny finally dropped, he would just smile and say, 'Good lad.'

Ben was very easy to sidetrack. Get him talking about a subject he was passionate about and he would talk for hours whilst we just sat on our benches doing nothing (which was the whole idea – it was like a sport to us!) I once remember getting through an entire lesson with him telling us about the influence that Queen Victoria had on fashion and the furniture of that era.

If at all possible he would have us make items without using any screws or nails. He trained us in the use of dove-tail joints and using dowels and glue to joint together pieces of wood. It has stood me well over the years. At least these days I can still make something that stays together!

When I was just coming up to being sixteen, I had started going out with a girl at school. I was in a free study period in our form room when Ben sent a first year with a message that he wanted to see me. I duly attended and he was alone in the workshop. He had a tray with a pot of tea and two cups. He said, 'Pull up a chair lad and let's have a chat.' He then poured me a cup of tea. This was entirely unheard of – I felt hugely privileged! He then went on to tell me that it had come to his attention that I had 'Started courting and walking out with a young lass' as he put it. Somewhat taken aback at the statement, I just nodded (almost spilling my tea down my shirt). He smiled gently and said, 'Don't be in a rush to grow up, lad.'

When I asked him what he meant he by that, he said that I should enjoy these golden days. He told me that I had all the time in the world to become a grown-up and just enjoy holding hands and going for a walk. Go and pick her some flowers – girls like that. I found it all very old-fashioned and comical at the time, but such was the respect I had for the man I never let it show.

It was only years later that it all dawned on me. He knew that Dad was ill and he took on the duty of having the kind of gentle chat that a dad would have with his son. He was being a sort of uncle to me. He wanted me to stay on the straight and narrow and not get into any trouble (or get my girlfriend in any trouble either!) He was quite an exceptional person was Ben. He was old-school but gentle and caring. I never saw him ever lose his temper or hit anyone. He would just tell us to go and sit in the wood room until we learned to behave. If I had been educated in one of the top public schools instead of the comprehensive I did attend, I would have had to go a long way to find another teacher of his calibre.

This wasn't to say that all the teachers were like that – far from it. I didn't breeze through school cosseted in some kind of rosy, supportive little cotton-wool world. Some teachers were just out-and-out thugs. A few were treading time until retirement, but we did have a small core of outstanding teachers that picked up the slack for the rest of them. I'm glad I didn't go to the school down the road that some of my friends went to. It was academically similar to my school, but the stories about the brutish way the teachers were with them made me appreciate our lot even more.

It was many years later that I heard the sad news that Ben had passed away. He was buried back in his beloved Yorkshire. If ever I am passing a joinery shop or smell wood being cut it always takes me back and thoughts of Ben usually spring to mind. I wonder if he knew how much he meant to us all?

1967 – One Man and his Horse

I sat upon a five bar gate one warm summer's afternoon to watch the hay-making taking place in the fields about a half mile away from where I lived. Rows of hay, straight standing in long rows fell like soldiers beneath the hungry mouth of the clattering old baler. Ruddy faced, tousle haired farm boys, pitchforks in hand, followed an old Fordson tractor, throwing bales onto the trailer it was towing. They did it effortlessly, as if they were feather pillows.

With hands like shovels, these oxen hearted sons of yeomen were magnificent. Their tanned bodies glistening with their honest sweat. They were like gladiators! Just then, I heard a voice behind me say, 'It was all different in my day.' I turned to see a local character we all knew as Old Jed. We both watched them. Old Jed filled and lit his pipe. Wisps of acrid smoke curling from the bowl of his much loved old briar. His thoughts seemed far away. I brought him back into the current world by saying, 'How was it different?'

His face softened a little, and he trawled through reminiscences of everything being done either by hand, by horse or with a traction engine that moved from farm to farm at harvest time. Then he went on to describe the parties they held in the farmyards after the hay-making. He spoke of summer dances and blushing milkmaids. Heavily booted farmhands, fleet of foot and happy hearted. Their steps floating, light as mosquitoes. Farm girls in their arms, gazing adoringly at their rural, bull-chested heroes.

He then went on to tell me of the wartime improvements of

farming and its practices. I could see it troubled him. He said that the country would have starved if they hadn't improved things, but went on to tell me about how the horses were no longer efficient enough and how they had to go. I naively asked if they were put out to pasture and he said, 'No lad'.

He told me about going into their stalls on cold winter evenings and grooming them. Their warm, contented bodies standing patiently as his brush swept across their coats that gleamed like newly fallen conkers. Their mouths pulling at their hay in their hay nets. He also told me about the knacker man taking them away. He could see that it probably wasn't a conversation to be held with a young lad, so he just said, 'All a long time ago, young fella,' and left it at that. It was a truth that didn't need saying!

Now, when I see these gentle giants at some agricultural show, or pulling a dray wagon. These fabulous, glossy beasts with hooves as big as dinner plates and their white-feathered fetlocks, I can't help but remember old Jed and his words on that day. They did everything for us, from pulling the plough to pulling cannons in the first world war. They are the gentlest and yet the most powerful of horses. Thank God we now value and cosset them. Without them we wouldn't have been the nation we are. When you have stood with a horse and gazed into the black orbs of its patient eyes, you may well understand the way that they can touch your soul. I have two little chaps and they have touched mine.

1968 – The Field Trip

The school had organised that the whole class was to head off to the countryside for a whole week in rural Lancashire. It was a purpose built centre that had seventy plus beds in a dormitory block and several outdoor activities. We were told that there was even a swimming pool. I really looked forward to going, but also felt a bit of trepidation, as this was the first time I had ever gone away without my parents. I would be around thirteen.

When we arrived we all went to our beds. They were lovely affairs, each set in their own cubicle with a bedside cupboard and lamp, plus a small wardrobe affair for our clothes. The cubicle had a curtain at the end of it for privacy. There was a shower block and a toilet at the end of the block. The girls had exactly the same, but one floor up. After stowing away all our gear we wanted to see the swimming pool.

We could see the swimming pool about twenty yards away. When we got there it was empty. It looked like it hadn't seen water for some time as it had dead leaves in it. It was bone dry – but, and it is a big but – it had a football in it, which had probably been left by the previous occupants. It made a perfect, self-contained, little five-a-side arena, and boy did it get some use!

We weren't there just for play. We had to go on treks through the countryside and look at trees and such (yawn), but they did take us to a local cave complex. We were each issued with a hard hat to stop us banging our heads on the cave roof, and we were led by a guide through the caves, all of which were tastefully floodlit to emphasise the wonderful stalactites and stalagmites. It was breathtaking. We even saw an underground lake that supposedly had fish in it!

We were accompanied by two teachers. One male and one female. The male teacher proved to be a bigger kid than all of us put together. He sent the girls out on some pretence or other – to collect pine cones for a class lecture I think it was, and we organised a raid on the girls dormitory.

Firstly we took out the boards on some of the beds, so that as soon as they lay on them the mattress would fall inwards. In some others we turned the sheet so that it only covered half the length of the bed. This meant that when they tried to slide their legs under the sheets, they would be stopped halfway down the bed. The one thing we did do to all of them though was to put itching powder that we had made from the insides of Burdock seed burrs inside every one of their nighties. All the above tricks were his suggestions. He also took out the spindle from their dormitory door, which meant that once the door was closed, it couldn't be opened, because the handles turned nothing inside – and the showers and toilets were on the far side!

All went hilariously as planned and every trick worked a treat. We all howled with laughter listening to them bang on the door shouting, 'Let us out, we are all itching to death!' One of the voices was that of the female teacher, and she certainly did not sound happy. We re-assembled the door handle mechanism and let them out. The female teacher gave her male colleague a withering look.

Some time later we heard her yelling at him. We couldn't hear it all but we heard such things as, 'Bloody big kid!' and 'At your age too...what are you....six???' He was making wheedling apologies and saying, 'It was just a bit of fun.' She made him take every one of their nighties down to a laundrette in the nearest village and wash them all at his own expense.

A day or so later, all the lads were in the swimming pool playing football. Someone shouted that lunch was ready. As we headed back we had to pass our dorms. One lad said, 'What are all those in our dorm windows?'

As we approached we could see that they had taped our underpants to the window. When we went to retrieve them, we saw that they had written insults across the back of our underpants in permanent marker, making uncomplimentary remarks about our manhood. We couldn't really complain. We really had asked for it.

In sheer bravado, we wore the defaced pairs of underwear over the top of our trousers in Superman fashion and walked like male models to our dining room tables to the whistles and jeers of the girls. Each one of us stopped in front of the female teacher and waved our bottoms at her so she could read the slogans.

She giggled and clapped like a schoolgirl.

A Kiss in the Park – 1970

On our first date we just walked and talked. I can't remember which one of us dared to reach out and hold the other's hand, but the soft and gentle wonderment of it sent a thrill through my body. You had such blue eyes. I think that is the one singular thing, in combination with that smile and those perfect lips that I so longed to kiss, that I fell in love with – and now those lips seemed within reach, but still so far away.

The discussions we had were wonderful. They ranged from school and the worries of our impending exams to the impossible dream that there was a life after school. A real life. This legend that bore the sombre name 'Career'. We ended up on a bench in the park, beside the flowers. As evening fell, the soft tendrils of a summer's moon reached down to bring our hearts to the surface and take our senses to within a small breath of complete intoxication. The smell of jasmine keeping our minds rooted there. We bathed in its grace, transfixed and wrapped in its unworldly beauty. We were completely in the grip of its guile.

Your hand took mine and brought me back with a delicious thrill of surprise. It's perfect isn't it? I whispered as if in some kind of church and within touching distance of God or a deity. You leaned across and kissed me and suddenly the world was complete. The softness and thrill of your lips that I had imagined for so long were a mocking travesty of the reality. I could never have imagined such a breathless, perfect madness of being lost so totally. Kidnapped and beguiled with the touch of your lips on mine. My arm reached around you instinctively to pull you closer to me. After we broke away from the kiss we rested our foreheads together in the relief that it had finally happened. It was a release and a jubilation.

You lifted your head and your smile said more than any piece of poetry ever dared. No words have ever been spoken about that kiss until now. It was one of those perfections that would have only been sullied by speech at the time it happened. Added to this, our young hearts and tender years couldn't have fully understood it all, let alone tried to encompass its feelings in mere words.

All these years later I can remember that kiss. If I close my eyes and concentrate, I can almost feel it. I can smell the jasmine and feel the warm breeze on my cheek. I can only stand so close to that fire for a few precious moments before having to go for a walk to shake off the past. I smile when I think about all that time that I admired you from afar. Hoping seemingly beyond hope that something unexpected would happen.

My Blessing to You

You are a small oasis of perfect sanity
when I am thirsty for understanding.
You make me cry without tears
and laugh within sorrow.
In my world I have saved a place
for your memory within my tired mind.
I remember wanting to find words.
I wanted to tell you
That you were my right hand
My sword of righteousness
My restful sleep and my joy of joys.
You meant that much my love
that sometimes I could bleed

from my very soul.
I hope I said all this
in a kiss.

D. Hayes 1997

1960s – The Market

I have never been to Morocco and strolled around a souk (some spell it souq) and taken in all the colourful and exciting sights. I have never bartered with anyone over the price of anything, especially something I wasn't particularly bothered about owning. I imagine I would be awful at it. The nearest I have come to experiencing this is the outdoor market that used to appear in our town twice a week (at least I think it was twice!).

It really came into its full majesty when it was an autumn or winter's late afternoon. Outside the stalls would hang strings of electric lights. Some were the old-school types and had paraffin lamps instead. It became almost like a film set. You could almost imagine Bill Sykes walking through with his dog, or the Artful Dodger stealing handkerchiefs from passing gentlemen. It had a fascination and a timeless wonderment to me. You could buy just about anything from there, and always cheaper than in the nearby shops (but certainly not always of a better quality). That was the whole thing about the adventure of it all. The words *Caveat Emptor* have never been spoken with more truth!

The subtly lit stalls and the shouts from the market vendors were an assault on the senses. We had one chap who sold crockery. He would say such things as, 'I will throw in twelve plates, twelve side plates, six cups and saucers. Am I asking five pounds like the big shops? – no I'm not!' He would then toss the whole bundle up in the air a little and catch it again without dropping a thing. The crowd

130

would gasp at this. 'All this for two quid, come on – get your purse out,' he would say to some old dear he had singled out. It was free entertainment. None of the 'Put your credit card in there Sir and enter your pin number'. This was theatre!

There were also the smells from the food stalls and the dazzling array of cakes, biscuits and sweets that were displayed attractively to tempt your taste buds. Mothers would tow their children around and try pairs of trousers against their uncooperative offspring whilst saying such things as, 'If you don't behave and keep still I will give you such a crack.' The stalls that sold loose sweets by the quarter were always the biggest draw to me. Two I remember especially were Cough Candy and Pear Drops. Oh how I loved Pear Drops – their tart, sharp taste and a vague smell of nail polish remover!

There were no old, plastic carrier bags blowing around in the breeze. Everything went into a paper bag, or was deposited directly into a shopping bag or basket. All prices were hand-written on bits of cardboard and placed in front of the article in question. 'Come and get your potatoes, fresh Jerseys just in!' the greengrocer would shout. It always confused me, as a jersey to me was a woollen jumper.

After your shopping expedition, you would head off towards the bus station. The stoic, headscarf-wearing women were struggling along like pack horses with two shopping bags in each hand. Once these ladies were on the bus, the conversations would start. 'How does your Billy like his new job?' and other such questions were bandied around and answered in full. Kids were chided and told to stop fidgeting. All of the characters of our own, home-grown soap opera would be represented on the leatherette seats of the bus.

The cheerful bus conductor would take the fares and turn a handle on his ticket machine to produce a ticket. They would say such things as, 'Don't put your shopping bag in the aisle, love. Someone might trip over it'. This would then be moved to in front of their feet. Probably without a break in the conversation they were having.

Eventually they decided to 'modernise' our town centre. A new Market Hall was built and the stalls were moved indoors. It was awful! It felt to me like trying to eat a Mars Bar without removing the wrapper. Every ounce of character, magic, and indeed pleasure had been sucked out of it and sanitised. Many never made the move as the stalls were quite expensive. Instead of the old outdoor market, they built a concrete and glass abortion that was our new library. Another bone of contention with me, but that is another story!

I had pride in my old town. It had charm and character. In the town centre modernisation, several buildings that in posh towns would have been Grade 1 listed buildings were swept aside to build shiny palaces to the Gods of retail. I don't go home too much these days. It is just far too painful.

1968 – The Motorbike

This story involves an old motorbike that was lying around in an old chap's back yard. It was underneath his kitchen window. It had been covered with an old tarpaulin and was just sitting there for donkey's years. One day (and probably after some pressure by his wife to take it to the tip) he decided to ask us if we wanted it. OF COURSE we wanted it!! It was an old BSA. After taking off the number plates (he didn't want any more association with it) he handed it over to us.

The next thing we did was wheel it round to Bernard's dad. He was a mechanic. He took one look at the bike and his face lit up. 'Bloody 'ell' he said 'I had one of them buggers'. We wheeled it round to his shed in the back yard and we all started tinkering with it. After draining off the petrol tank and re-filling it with fresh petrol, Bernard's dad set about replacing the spark plug. This done, he mounted the bike, thrust down the kick-start with his foot a couple of times and it miraculously pulsed into life. We all danced with joy.

Bernard's dad then issued us all with a stern warning about it being illegal to even push it on the streets without tax and insurance. He then told us a few stomach-churning stories about head injuries he had seen in motorbike accidents. He opened a cupboard in his shed and brought out an old crash helmet. One of those with a peak on it like they had in the 50s. He said, 'keep off the streets and go into the fields. Whoever is riding it, put the skid-lid on,' which was an old slang term for a crash helmet.

Ten minutes later we were on the derelict land at the back of the colliery. This land backed on to a row of semi-detached houses and their back gardens. I had never ridden a motorbike before. Bernard's dad had shown us all where the clutch was and how the foot-operated gear lever worked. We kicked the bike into life and I got on. The crash helmet could be described as 'a bit of a loose fit'. It kept sliding down over my eyes. I revved the engine, selected a gear (I thought it was first gear) and released the clutch lever and the bike did a wheelie and threw me straight into a muddy puddle.

All my friends were physically rolling around on the floor, convulsed with laughter. Bernard said, 'Give us the helmet and let me show you how it's done'. He threw his leg over the bike, selected a gear, balanced the engine and clutch and moved away as smoothly as a professional. Soon he was flying down the path. We all watched in admiration.

It came to our notice that at the end of this particular path was one of those ponds that was about three inches deep in water but about a foot deep in black, oozing mud. We all asked each other the question, 'Did anyone try the brakes?' – and none of us had. We heard the engine noise drop down to a pop, pop, pop instead of the high-pitched whine it had previously been, but Bernard still seemed to be travelling along at the same speed as previously. The next thing we saw – his legs were no longer on the footrests, but were flailing around as the bike weaved crazily from side to side. The next thing we witnessed was him disappearing out of sight, followed a split second later by a splash and a plume of black mud.

By the time we had caught up with him we were all relieved to see that he had managed to throw the bike onto its side, short of the edge, before throwing himself off and straight into the pond. He looked like The Creature From the Black Lagoon. Little Tony (who was called little because he was actually very tall for his age – don't ask, I suppose you had to be there) made the innocent remark, 'Oh that's good, you kept the bike out of the pond.' Bernard promptly hit him right on the nose.

A couple of days (and a few more minor spills and thrills) later, we all got fairly proficient at riding the bike. We had fixed the brakes (a simple matter of putting the brake cables back on to their fixings – oops!). We decided we would plot a course round all the little paths that led off in all directions across the wasteland and we would have a time trials. Bernard was all pumped up and ready for this. We were still singing songs from *The Black and White Minstrel show* at him and calling him 'Mammy' after the Al Jolson song. He had a point to prove!

It came his turn and he set off like a man possessed. The engine whined as he wobbled it around the corners, skidding his foot on the floor like they did at the speedway track. Unfortunately he came to grief as he was heading for the semi-detached houses. He mis-timed the corner and he and the bike skidded sideways across the floor and straight through a picket fence surrounding one of the gardens. The handlebars had made a beautiful scimitar-shaped mark straight across the lawn. He had then cut a small, concrete statue completely in half with the bike before coming to rest under the house owner's patio furniture.

We didn't run away despite us all wanting to. We were all responsible really; we all had to pay for the damage. This included having the fence replaced. The owner let us off with the statue as he said (in his words), 'I never liked the bugger anyway, it was the wife's idea'.

The original owner must have been getting grief from all the neighbours. He came to find us and took back the bike. He put it back beneath his kitchen window and put the tarpaulin over it again. There it stayed for years before we finally saw it in a skip outside his house in bits. A sad end to a fine machine.

1968 – The Birds and the Bees

I would be approaching my thirteenth birthday. It was the first period of the afternoon and we had Biology. We all shuffled into the science lab and arranged ourselves at our seats. In strode Mr Moffatt – a very pleasant chap in his mid thirties, with a ruddy complexion and a shock of auburn hair on his head. He looked as if something was mildly worrying him.

He cleared his throat and announced, 'Today we will be dealing with reproduction.' He then scrolled the blackboard down to reveal a penis in cross section. We hardly dared believe what we were seeing. Barry asked the question, 'Is that a willie sir?' He said that it was indeed what might be called a willie, but its proper name was penis. Just by hearing him say the words was enough to cause little pockets of chuckling to break out. 'Okay,Okay, settle down. Let's try and be grown-up about this,' he said. Grown up about it? – no chance! This was brilliant. We were going to wring out every last drop of fun.

He went on to describe the reproduction process in a very clinical way. He used words like 'erection', which caused Barry to turn to us and say, 'He means a stiffie,' which had us all chuckling. Mr Moffatt's voice boomed out, 'I won't tell you again, and Barry – face the front and take that smirk off your face.' His own face began to resemble the colour of his hair in a combination of a blush and mild irritation.

The girls didn't seem to find it quite as funny as we did, but there were plenty of embarrassed giggles coming from them. He scrolled down the blackboard to reveal yet another picture. It was a cross section of the female reproductive organs. Someone said, 'It looks like a cow's head' and someone else said, 'It's like something off Dr Who.' Peals of laughter followed the remarks. Barry turned to the class and said, 'Well I've seen my sister's, and it looks nothing like that'. Well, that was it; the class was rolling around with laughter. Mr Moffatt totally lost it and barked at us all, 'SHUT UP, JUST SHUT UP OR ALL OF YOU WILL BE IN DETENTION – AND YOU BARRY, GET OUT, GET OUT BOY!' Mr Moffatt's head now positively glowed bright red and he was now sporting a prominent vein on his forehead. He turned to the rest of the class and said, in a low and menacing voice, 'One more bloody comment from any of you and I swear I will swing for the little bugger that makes it'.

Composure was restored and the rest of the lesson was carried out in relative calm. When the bell went, I saw Mr Moffatt slump down into his chair. He was now looking slightly pale and somewhat weary. He told us all to leave quietly. As I walked out of class I heard Mr Moffatt say in a sorrowful voice, 'I need a sodding drink.'

I saw him later on in the day. He was chatting with a few of his colleagues who found his story quite amusing. The maths teacher patted him on the shoulder and said, 'Rather you than me old chap, rather you than me'. Mr Moffatt nodded in solemn agreement.

I met him many years later. He was pushing a trolley around a supermarket. I approached him and said, 'You probably don't remember me, but you taught me biology.' He said he did remember who I was, but possibly he was just being kind. When I mentioned the sex education lesson and Barry, his face broke out into a big grin. 'Oh that little sod,' he said, 'I remember him.' He went on to tell me that most years he taught reacted quite similarly, but our particular class, mainly due to Barry, had been a memorable one. I hope he has had a long and a happy retirement. If any teacher deserved it, it was him!

Late 60s - Sleeping Rough

Dad used to tell us tales of when he and his brothers would head off camping. They had a couple of tarpaulins and a rope, and a ball of sisal string for the guy ropes. The idea was that the rope was fastened between two trees and the tarpaulin thrown over it. The sisal was tied through the loop holes and fastened to hand-made tent pegs that they had made from willow branches. Once the guy ropes were stretched tight it gave the tarpaulin the shape of a tent. Beneath this was placed the second tarpaulin as a sleeping area to keep out any ground moisture.

He told us how to make the pegs using a jack knife and to take a mallet to hammer them in. He told us they would take a storm lantern like the one we hang in the outside toilet and a bike lamp each. They would take a tin plate each and a saucepan to cook the beans in over a fire. A bottle of water and some cups, A box of matches, and an old pillowcase that they would fill with hay from a local farm. That would be their pillow. They also took an army blanket each.

Our little gang met up and I relayed the information to them as to what was needed. We had already decided to do this in a totally authentic manner. We didn't want our Dads being able to downgrade any of our efforts. If it wasn't available back then, it wasn't used now! We all filled our backpacks (freshly purchased from the good old Army and Navy Stores) with all necessary supplies. The tarpaulins were borrowed from the Dad of one of our lads in our gang. Off we set into the wilds. To be exact, the woods near The Flash (a lake) about a mile away.

When we arrived, we found two likely looking trees and tied the rope between them. We threw the 'Tarp' over it and fastened the sisal guy ropes to it. We then set off to find willow to use for the tent pegs. This is where our planning began to unravel. None of us knew what willow looked like, so we just chose any old tree. We made the pegs and tapped them into the ground with half a brick (because one of the lads had forgotten the mallet that he said he would bring). When we tied the string to the pegs, under any sort of pressure from the string, the pegs would snap. We abandoned this idea and just tied the strings to the surrounding trees. Some of the guy ropes must have been fifteen feet long.

Once this was done we placed the second 'tarp' onto the ground. We all agreed that this looked very cosy indeed! We hadn't managed to find a local farm, so we stuffed the pillow cases with dried grass and leaves instead of fresh, fragrant hay. Consequently they stank like a woodland floor. We gathered together some wood for the fire, and fortunately we found some old newspaper to get the kindling started. Soon the fire was roaring happily away. Now, what was it that Dad said about positioning the fire? Oh that was it. Make sure the smoke was blowing AWAY from the tent....oops!

We settled in and felt like pioneers. Soon the saucepan came out and a big tin of beans. 'Did anyone bring a tin opener?' I asked. Apparently no one had. We opened the tin of beans with the jack knife and the half brick we had used to hammer in the pegs. The contents of the bean tin was poured into the saucepan and it was balanced on the fire. Soon it was bubbling away merrily. We all got out our little tin plates in readiness. Someone then asked who had brought the spoons. No one apparently! One lad stood up and said 'Sod this' and he kicked the saucepan off the fire and said he was off to the chippy. We all gave him our money and soon he was back with our chips.

Just as it was going dusk one of the lads' older brothers came to check out our progress. He was quite impressed at the camp we had made. He even said 'I see by the empty tin and dirty saucepan you have had beans as well'. None of us contradicted him!

He sat by the fire with us and lit a cigarette. He then said, 'You do know about the drowned boy don't you?' We all said that we didn't. 'Oh aye,' he said. 'He drowned right over there in the flash. He sank to the bottom and was trapped in the weeds. He wasn't found for over a week. He then went on to tell us that he (the drowned boy) didn't like anyone being around there after nightfall as his spirit would wander up and down the bank. He would be shouting 'Mummy, Mummy, I can't find you, Mummy'. We all looked at each other in fear and trepidation. One of the lads said 'That sounds like a load of crap.' The older brother stubbed out his cigarette and said, 'Well don't say I didn't warn you,' then he left.

As night fell we were acutely aware of every noise, no matter how slight. We kept the fire healthily stoked with fuel. One lad said 'I want the toilet'. We told him to take a pee in the bushes. He then said 'No, I want the toilet... properly.' We told him that he had better take some of the chip paper with him and just go in the bushes. So he did. Now what was it that Dad said about this?' oh yes. As with the fire, make sure the wind is blowing away from the tent, and don't do it in a bush ten feet upwind of the tent, like he had.

'God almighty, that poo stinks,' one of the lads said. Another answered, 'Well it would, it's poo.' For some odd reason we all found it hilarious. I think it was a reaction to the fact that we were all 'bricking it'. The only comfort, if any, was in knowing that at least one of us had empty bowels!

It would be approaching eleven thirty when one of the lads said, 'Can you hear that?' We all stopped and listened. We could hear a faint, reedy little noise. At first, we couldn't catch what it was. One of the lads said, 'I think it said Mummy.' We were willing to believe him too! With some trepidation we ventured forth to discover the source of the noise. It turned out not to be a voice at all, but a fisherman who was out for a spot of night fishing. It was the creaking of the basket he sat upon.

We got back to our little camp and the security of our paraffin lamp and settled down for the night. We were a little happier knowing that there was an adult thirty yards away. A slight breeze had started up which blew straight underneath the tarpaulin. We were freezing, but at least we could no longer smell the crap in the bushes. We managed to get a little sleep, but as soon as there was enough light to dismantle camp, we did. We were all mentally and physically trashed. We trudged home and made straight for our beds, but not before having a nice cup of tea – as we hadn't taken a kettle and tea bags with us either!

The next day Dad told me that they only ever went in the baking heat of summer, and that he had lied about stuffing the pillow with hay. They took a real pillow each. Oh and they used proper tent pegs. I sat aghast listening to him atone for his lies. He also told me that they didn't cook beans on an open fire, but went to the chippy and also called in at the pub for some bottles. He then praised me for 'doing it properly'. I didn't dispel the myth by saying that we had bought chips too.

Just Sitting Still

We adored the countryside, and we were quite well blessed with a variety of different habitats, from arable farmland to old, disused, Victorian mining sites. There were also little woods and copses around and a scattering of wetlands. They held a variety of birds and animals. A friend and I would build a makeshift hide out of old sacks and garden canes. Once the canes were pressed into the ground and the sacks draped over them,we would cover the old sacks with twigs and dried grasses and sit inside the makeshift shelters. We would peer through a couple of holes that we had cut into the sacks about the size of our fists.

I had saved up for a pair of 8x40 binoculars that were in a second-hand shop. They were my pride and joy. I felt like a real naturalist and ornithologist. We would pack a flask and some sandwiches and spend a whole afternoon, just moving around from location to location. Whenever I spotted anything of interest we would share the binoculars, taking turns in looking at it. I still have an old *Observers Book of British Birds* from those days. Each bird inside the book that we had seen has a tick against it. Some we would never see if we sat there forever. There weren't any Capercaillie around the Northwest of England, and the nearest Dartford Warbler would be some four hundred miles or so away.

We saw all kinds of things, though. We sat as still as rocks, hardly daring to breathe, and waited to see what ventured out in front of us. We once saw a weasel busying itself, searching through the undergrowth not twenty yards away. We had never seen a weasel before that day. We saw the occasional stoat and plenty of rabbits.

We managed to find a fox's den and set up our hide well before dark, around twenty yards away from the fox hole. We went there night after night. It was only on the fourth night that we saw a pair of foxes emerge from the den and scurry off to hunt. We must have seen them for all of ten seconds, but it was enough. We had seen them, and that was all that mattered!

Eventually we graduated to a tent that was green in colour already, but which we then draped the sacks and leaves over the top of it. It made it almost invisible to anyone casually passing by. We would make good use of available cover. We would camp out overnight in our little den, and fall asleep to the sounds of barn owls screeching. One night we were awoken by what we at first thought was a girl screaming like she was being murdered. We crept out of our tent and searched the area, but found no dead bodies. We later found out that it was the noise a fox makes to announce its presence. It certainly gave us the creeps that first time we heard it. We would hear it quite regularly on other outings.

It was here I learned how to knock together a meal. We had a primus stove with us and a couple of pots and pans. I would fry up bacon and eggs in a frying pan, or we would have baked beans. We couldn't have both at the same time as we only had one primus. We usually had bacon, eggs and baked beans, but in two separate sittings. The bacon and eggs first, followed by the beans. After that, the kettle would go on and we would have a nice brew.

Food tastes so much nicer in the outdoors. We would crudely wash our plates down by pouring water from the water bottle we had brought, whilst scrubbing them with dried grass. I can't say it got them spotlessly clean, but it was close enough for us! We didn't have al fresco dining such as this all the time. It was a short enough walk to the pie shop, where we would purchase hot meat and potato pies (or potato and meat as we now must call them!). There was also the chippy or the newsagents where we could buy Eccles cakes, crisps and chocolate. Let's just say that we didn't starve!

We would carry on these activities at weekends well into October. We once had the idea of camping out in mid December, but we didn't even last out the night. We were freezing. We thought of lighting a fire, but what would be the point of that? We wouldn't see much afterwards by the way of wildlife. The next time we went was the following May.

Mid 60s – Smoking

Quite a few young lads of my era were experimenting with smoking. In those days you could buy five cigarettes and a book of matches. Virtually any shop would just hand them over to you – no questions asked. If you were asked you would merely say, 'They are for me Dad,' and the goods would be handed over to you.

Most smoking first occurred as experimentation. Most adults smoked back then. It was almost a rite of passage to 'spark up your first fag'. I remember cigarettes being passed around within groups of boys (and some girls) almost like marijuana. The recipients taking a few puffs before passing the cigarette on to the next in line. We were asked to smoke with dry mouths by someone saying, 'Don't make a duck's arse of it.' meaning don't get the end wet and flatten it.

I had tried cigarettes, but to me they were horrible. The smoke made my mouth taste awful for ages after, and I even disliked the smell of them on other people. Dad smoked a pipe. He smoked a tobacco that Mam bought for him at the Co-op called 'Mahogany Flake'. I loved the smell of it.

Dad had several old pipes in a drawer that he never smoked. The tobacco residue in them smelled lovely to me, and they were such tactile and beautiful objects. One pipe was my particular favourite. It was a curly pipe – the stem being carved to look like a leg with a footballer's boot. On the boot was balanced a football with the top cut off it. This made the bowl. I took this and another straight briar and put them in my pocket.

I didn't want to go to the Co-op to buy Dad's (and my) favourite brand as Mam was too well known in there. It wouldn't take long before someone told her I had been buying tobacco, so I went to a local newsagent. I said to the shopkeeper, 'I have come to buy Dad some pipe tobacco for his birthday.' The shopkeeper asked me what he smoked. When I told him 'Mahogany Flake' he told me that this was something the Co-op made for themselves. He then offered me a tin of St Bruno saying that it was very similar. I bought it and left the shop.

Some time later, I met up with Geoff and showed him my ill-gotten goods. We had arranged to go fishing, so off we went to a local mill lodge. We set up our rods and cast in our floats, and I broke out the pipes and tobacco. Soon we were engulfed in clouds of acrid, blue smoke. We were chuffing away merrily, stopping occasionally to spit.

It didn't take long before I started to feel dizzy and a little bit sick. I turned to look at Geoff and he too had gone a pale and delicate shade of green. Within a minute we were both projectile vomiting into the grass. I have never felt quite so bad. It took ages for my head and stomach to settle down. I opened the tobacco tin and emptied the contents into the water. 'Bugger that,' I said, and Geoff whole-heartedly agreed.

I deposited Dad's pipes back in the drawer from whence they came. I am breaking my silence on this after some fifty years by telling you this story; it has been a secret between Geoff and me. We told no one. It was hardly one of our most glorious moments after all!

I suppose that in a way it had been a good lesson to us both. Neither of us consequently went on to smoke in our youth. Ironically I did take up smoking in my early twenties and smoked a pipe. I mistakenly thought that it made me look more colourful and interesting to the ladies – it didn't. I was quite quickly informed that

I looked like a pensioner. Friends of both sexes told me to go outside and take the vile, stinking thing with me. Some girls would be more succinct with their insults and would merely walk by and say, 'Tosser.' I only smoked in private after that. I soon gave up. It was expensive! Added to this was the inconvenience of the whole thing. You needed a whole armoury of items to smoke a pipe. The pipe itself, the tobacco wallet, a pipe knife, a lighter and possibly a couple of pipe cleaners. I found my pockets bulged with smoking equipment. The pipe had to go! – I ended up just leaving everything on a table inside a pub on purpose and just walking away. Hopefully the landlord found them and donated them to some old chap. Whatever he did with them, I was glad to see the back of them!

The Bouncer

As an adolescent, absolutely nothing was sacred. We would make fun of everything, with one notable exception – ourselves. We took ourselves very seriously indeed! The only good music was the music we listened to. Everything else was crap. Yeah, that's right CRAP!! We would sit round on the floor in Mam's front room in the dark, listening to records really loudly....Okay, not too loudly as Mam would tell us to turn it down – and it wasn't really dark as we had a street lamp right outside our house. So to be more accurate, we sat in Mam's front room bathed in a glaring orange glow, listening to music at a moderate level.

Being LP's – or for any younger readers, long playing vinyl records played at thirty three and a third revolutions; they lasted for ages. To be precise, about twenty-five minutes per side. Once the record had finished, the needle would enter the end groove of the record and the speakers would make the hisssss pop hisssss pop noise until someone got up off the floor and removed the stylus arm and turned the record over.

I once asked a friend during one of these nocturnal record playing sessions the question, 'How cool are we?'. He said, 'We are cooler than a bucket of penguin shit.' Not knowing the ambient temperature of penguin guano, I took this to mean that we were very cool. Happy with the answer, we sank back down on to Mam's half wool, half polyester carpet and listened to Jethro Tull. The

148

conversation was usually about girls – or the lack of them!

We decided that our coolness wasn't in any doubt, but maybe a bunch of adolescent boys listening to records with the lights switched off in the front room of a council house in the north west wasn't quite what would attract girls. In fact, it looked quite gay. We decided that the world was ready for our dazzling wit and consummate dress sense, so decided that the next night we were going to head down to the dance hall.

It was Saturday night and we confidently walked up to the door of the local Palais. Something that approximated a shaved gorilla in a dinner jacket stopped us with a hand the size of a dinner plate. 'Bugger off!' it barked at us. When we asked why, he used immaculate logic and reason, and described the situation to us in the clearest of terms. He said, 'Because if you don't I will knock effing big holes through you, tear your heads off, and shit down your necks.' We could have argued with him and forced our way past him, but there were three of us, and it wouldn't have been fair would it?

We were going to go home when we decided that we might as well call in for a drink at a pub. We pushed open the door of the nearest pub and strode up to the bar. The barman said 'Is it bob-a-job week so soon?' When we asked him what he meant he said, 'Well I can't think of any other reason for a bunch of kids being inside a pub can you?' We didn't even bother arguing. To add insult to injury, a bunch of girls in my class at school were inside the pub. They spotted us and said, 'You sad little bastards!' and laughed. Perfect end to a perfect night.

We headed home and called in at an off licence to see if we could buy a big bottle of cider. I approached the man behind the counter and said, 'A bottle of Strongbow please.' He asked me if I was old enough. I had reached my breaking point, and said to him in a low and menacing voice, 'Well I wouldn't be asking for the pissing thing if I wasn't now would I? – Give me the Strongbow'. He said, 'OK, keep your hair on, Jimi Hendrix. I have to ask is all.' He handed over the bottle and we paid for it and headed back to my house.

Once home, Mam opened the door (as she didn't trust me with a key) and let us in. 'You are all back early aren't you?' Mam said. 'I thought you were going to a dance?'. I told her we were bored with it so we came home. 'Oh, they wouldn't let you in then?' she said. I mumbled something about talking rubbish and to stop picking on me, and of course, that I hated her. All my friends said 'Hello Mrs Hayes' as they filed in past her.

We assembled ourselves on the carpet again and put some Neil Young on the record turntable. We left the lights on as we didn't want to spill the cider in the dark. I distributed some glasses between us and we drank cider. Neil Young sang, 'See the lonely boy, out on a weekend, trying to make it pay.' One of our bunch said, 'Switch that rubbish off – he is pissing me off.' The irony of the song wasn't lost on us either, so we put some Groundhogs on instead – and the talk was still about girls, or the lack of them.

1966 – Up in the Air

I don't know if they have them in other areas, but in the 60s we had travelling fairgrounds that moved from town to town. They would set up camp and all their rides on some piece of spare ground and usually stay for about a week. They were places of fascination and wonder to us kids, especially at night time when all the coloured bulbs would light up the sky, and also our imaginations.

As you approached, you could hear the diesel generators purring and the sound of music being played on the rides, interspersed with the screams from the girls as they were being twirled round and round by some denim-clad young man on the Waltzer. Then there were the delicious smells. The Hot Dog sellers, the Candy Floss and Toffee Apple stall and the Black Peas stand (my favourite). It was an exciting assault upon the senses. All the rides were there. The Caterpillar, The Waltzer, The Dodgems, and my favourite, The Big Wheel.

It was on one such visit to the fair that a friend and I queued to go on the big wheel. We sat in our seat and he pulled the bar down in front of us. We then moved up a place at a time so other people could join the ride and fill the remaining seats. This was a part of the exciting build up to the actual ride itself. Soon we were occupying a position close to the top spot and we could see right across the funfair. We could see the roofs of the shops and the smoking chimneys of the surrounding houses.

After a couple of minutes we hadn't moved. We thought that

perhaps they were waiting for enough people to fill up the ride, but when we looked down we could see a long queue. To our alarm we then saw a man speaking to the queue and they all turned away and left. Had they forgotten we were here? We then noticed people in the seats below us, so we knew this couldn't be the case.

It turned out that the small engine that ran the ride had seized and wisps of smoke could be seen issuing forth from it. We could see two or three men gesturing and arguing. They then left. We hoped it was to get help. By this time the wind had whipped up, making the little seat sway to and fro. It had also started to rain. We only had our jumpers on and we were freezing.

Some time later, a man arrived with a toolbox and started dismantling the engine. This didn't look like a small job! I heard the sound of the music from The Waltzer playing 'Hang on Sloopy'. If I had known what irony was at that age the humour of it would have helped. We had been up in the air for around an hour and the engine was still in bits. After drinking bottles of pop earlier on we were desperate to pee.

About ten minutes later, we saw a man arrive with a sledge hammer. He started to swing it at some piece of machinery and, after a couple of hefty blows, we then heard him say, 'That's got it.' They then started to pull the big wheel round by hand, letting the stranded passengers off. They got to us and we finally got off. My friend asked for our money back (which was sixpence). He gave us two shillings each. I suppose by way of some kind of compensation and in the hope we wouldn't go complaining to the authorities. We popped behind one of the wagons and had a well-earned pee.

Once we were back on Terra Firma, we felt fine. The rain had stopped and we were sheltered from the wind. We also had two bob each to spend. A bonus! We headed towards The Caterpillar. Anyone who hasn't seen this particular ride, it is a strange thing. It is a series of carriages that are all joined together. They trundle around a circular, undulating track. After a while a canvas canopy slides over the top of the passengers and they are in darkness. A fan beneath the tracks blows air into the carriages, lifting the girls' skirts and making them squeal. Those with ulterior motives loved The Caterpillar!

After having a go on The Dodgems and the Shooting Gallery, we bought ourselves a candy floss each and made our way the mile or so home. As we walked through the gloomy streets it felt like someone had turned off all the colours. A few days later and the local newspaper had an article on the front page. It was all about The Big Wheel breaking down and some lurid headline along the lines of *'Terrified passengers trapped on ride of terror'*. We hadn't been in the least terrified. We'd just wanted a pee!

Legless

It was just after my sixteenth birthday. A girl and I had made arrangements to meet up at my place and listen to some records and spend a cosy night in. She was around half an hour late, so I nipped out to the phone box (we didn't have a phone) to see if she was still coming round. The weather was atrocious – almost blizzard conditions. She picked up the phone and she said that she had better stay in as her mum didn't like her travelling on a night like this (fair comment really as she did have about five miles to travel by bus). I went home and shook the snow off my clothes and went into the front room. I had bought a cheap bottle of white wine (if you can call it that) by the name of Don Cortez – a particularly fine (ropey) vintage Spanish white wine. Being unaccustomed to how much wine you poured into a glass, I just chose a sizeable tumbler from the cocktail cabinet and filled it to the brim. After the first tarty hit from the wine, my tongue became almost anaesthetised. I found I didn't mind the taste, so I set about it with some gusto. I drank it like lemonade. After about an hour and a half the bottle was empty.

I decided to go into the living room and watch a bit of telly with my mum. As I was watching the TV, it seemed to keep leaping to the left, and I had to concentrate harder and harder to keep focus. Mum took one look at me and said, 'Have you been drinking?' I said, 'A bit.' When she asked what a bit was and I told her it was a bottle of wine, she rolled her eyes and said, 'Get to bed – I don't want to have to carry you upstairs.' So off I went, and not a minute too soon. By the time I reached the top of the stairs the room was spinning. I managed to get stripped off ready for bed and made a valiant attempt at putting on my pyjamas – a dreadful mistake! One leg of my pyjama trousers was the right way out and the other one was inside-out. After slipping my legs inside them (after much hopping around and stumbling into the wardrobe a couple of times) I tried to pull them up. Much to my amazement, the button was at the front but the button-hole was at the rear. I gave one almighty tug at the button-hole end in a crazed attempt at trying to bring it to the front, and at that moment the little sheepskin rug I was standing on slid from beneath me. I didn't so much fall in my mind – I was just astounded to find that the floor had come up to smack me in the face. BOOM... the house shook. Try as I might I couldn't get up. My legs were now like string. The next thing I saw was mother standing over me, mumbling something about 'just like his bloody dad'. She then had to dress her only son and tuck him up in bed. She had also brought a bucket up with her and placed it at the side of the bed. When I asked her what the bucket was for, she just said, 'You'll see.' – and do you know... I did see about half an hour later.

1962 – The Visit of One of My Uncles

On very rare occasions we were honoured with a visit from one of my Uncles. This one in question was my dad's brother. I won't directly name him for reasons that will become apparent in this story. I used to love his visits. They were always punctuated with a string of stories that used to mildly annoy my Dad. He used to say, after his visits, 'He can't even lie straight in bed – he talks a load of garbage.' The rest of us loved his stories though.

Using today's words, he would be classed as a huge bull-merchant. But to us he was a weaver of implausible tales – a story-teller supreme. The lurid tales and stories he told us kept us all in raptures. One time he pointed at his long-suffering wife and said, 'Tell them about your gall stones.'

She said, 'Why don't you tell them instead?'. So he did!

He said, 'They took out her gall stones and the doctors said that they had never seen anything like them.' When we asked why, he told us that they were massive. He picked up a sizeable orange from the fruit bowl on the sideboard and said, 'See this?' We all nodded.

He said, 'Her gall stones were bigger than this.'

My auntie just sighed softly and said, 'Now come on,' but to no avail – he had the floor and was in full, majestic flow. He became more flamboyant and animated as his performance unfolded. He then went on to tell us that they would be worth a fortune had he insisted on keeping them, but they had been sent to America for their top professors and doctors to look at, and they said that they had sent them back, but they must have been lost in the post!!

A little later he asked me the question, 'Do you still go fishing, David?' I said that I did. He then went on to regale us all with the story of a big carp he once hooked in the canal.

I asked him how big it was. He said, 'BIG....how BIG was it? – I'll tell you how big it was.' He was waving his arms around in excitement. He then went on to inform us that this carp was so big that it couldn't turn round in the straight sections of the canal, but had to go down to one of the basins that the barges used to turn round in, to be able to turn round itself.

I found myself actually applauding gleefully. This was a real, vintage, solid gold piece of absolute crap. Truly one of his finest!

He was also a St John's First Aid volunteer and a scout leader. One of my particular favourites of his was about one such scouting adventure. He said that he took a troop of 4000 scouts out into the Welsh Mountains for a weekend's camping. A complete pack of lies of course, but this never mattered to us. My Mam (ever the practical one) said to him, 'I bet they took some feeding.' He then went on to tell us that they took with them 56lb sacks of cornflakes and 50 gallons of milk. Try fitting that in a rucksack!

He then went on to tell us that one of his 'guards' had reported to him that the scout camp was about to come under attack from a marauding gang of ruthless Hell's Angels. He told us that he had dispersed all the scouts (or his troops as he called them) into a circle around the valley that they were camping in. He then told them to wait for his signal and they were all to turn on their torches and shine the lights down into the camp where the Hell's Angels were riding their motorcycles bent on death and destruction. He told us that all the torches came on in unison and the marauding gang was so terrified, they fled in fear of their lives.

By the time this particular story had finished, Dad was outside, sitting in the garden and quietly seething. He was smoking his pipe with a vengeance and was surrounded by his own private smog.

A little later, Uncle announced that they had better make a move if they wanted to avoid the traffic. Dad and his brother said their goodbyes by merely saying each other's name. Both nodded towards each other and my Aunt and Uncle got into their car and drove away with all of us waving them off cheerily (except Dad of course).

Uncle died a couple of years after this visit. He was only 51. With him had died our great storyteller. A great entertainer and raconteur. We can all moralise about it being wrong to lie, but I think he was aware that we didn't believe a word of any of his stories. They were harmless tales from the lips of a craftsman of the tall tale. They were small pieces of art in their own right. I have known the passing of quite a few such characters. This is why I write today – to try in my small way to immortalise them!

1962 to Present Day – The Brass Cat

On my desk sits a pair of brass cats. Probably dating to the mid 20th century and not worth very much. One has been with me since being around seven years old. So what? you might say, and I would agree. Why should odd bits of stuff lying around on my desk interest anyone? Allow me to try and explain.

Nanna's kitchen had a lovely old range with a mantelpiece above it, and on it were a few random bits of brass. A little bell shaped like a lady in a crinoline dress, a brass shell case from World War 1 that was used as a spill vase, a matchbox holder and a brass cat. I always asked if I could play with the brass cat, and Nanna would bring it down from the mantelpiece for me to play with.

Nanna's kitchen was somewhere I felt warm and safe. It was my second home. I went there daily. She had so many interesting things from a bygone era.

I invented a game with the brass cat where I used the flagstones on her kitchen floor as a sort of giant ludo board. I had a cotton reel and the brass cat. I would throw a dice and move the cotton reel along from stone to stone, then throw the dice for the cat. The idea of the game was that the cat was chasing a mouse. If the cat caught up before it reached the kitchen door then it had caught the mouse. If it didn't, the mouse had escaped. A simple game, but it entertained me for hours. If Nanna were to ask me what I was playing, I would say, 'I'm playing *Tom and Jerry*, Nanna.'

Nanna also had a few old rolls of wallpaper. I had pencils and crayons and could use bits of the wallpaper to draw on. Often, I would trace around the outline of the cat and then colour in the resulting shape. I coloured in black cats, stripey cats, whatever took my fancy. I also just appreciated it for what it was. It had a happy smile (I was later to find out that it was the grinning Cheshire Cat from *Alice in Wonderland*). It was also very tactile. I loved the feel of its brass curves.

One day Nanna announced that since I played with it so much I had better have it. I was made up. I gave her a big hug and said, 'Thanks Nanna.' She asked me what I was going to call it and I said, 'Cat.' She laughed and said, 'Well, at least you didn't stay up all night thinking of a name.'

'Cat' has been a constant throughout my life. It was on my bedside table as a kid, and it has moved with me wherever I have gone. It was in my coat pocket when I took my driving test, though it did lose its shine a little, as it took me three attempts to pass. It even followed me to hospital when I had to have an operation. When packing to move house, I have always just slipped Cat into my pocket so that it didn't get lost in the move. It is worth pennies, but to me it's my magic touchstone. My lucky charm.

So, here it sits on my desk. A little amulet. A reminder of Nanna's kitchen. A tangible aide memoire of the happy, loving days spent there. It also stands as a reminder that I had, and still have an imagination and I should use it more often. When I go through trying times (as do we all) its grinning face seems to say, 'Come on, don't be a miserable bugger.' It doesn't always work first time, but eventually it wears me down, so I have to grin back.

A couple of years ago, my partner had been to one of her regular forays to a local charity shop. I sat down at my desk to see two identical brass cats. She said to me, 'I've bought it a little friend to play with.'

I thanked her very much and said it was a lovely thought. It then struck me... which one was MY cat?? After much close examination, I gave up and decided that I couldn't tell, so I now have two brass cats. I have made up my mind that it isn't the actual object, but what it represents. I still have 'Cat' but I am just unsure as to which one it is! I am contented in the fact that it is a memory that is enshrined in brass, and now I have a spare one!

Holidays in the 60s

We didn't go on holiday every year. Some years were tighter than others money-wise. When we did decide to go, our destination of choice would be the North Wales coast. Usually around the Rhyl, Towyn and Abergele areas. We would have booked in to one of the holiday camps, usually Winkups or Golden Sands and hired a chalet or a caravan. We would have previously bought a return ticket from our local coach hire people and we would wait at the designated spot on a street corner.

There were dozens waiting with us, all with suitcases and bags, and mothers holding on to kids in various stages of excitement. The coach would pull up and we would all advance upon the driver with our suitcases, and he would bark at us, 'One at a time, I only 'ave one pair of bleedin' hands!' Soon all our luggage was safely stored aboard.

The holiday started the second we set foot on the coach (or charabanc as Mam always called it). If the weather was sunny and warm (and it always seemed to be in those halcyon times) the temperature inside the coach would be somewhere approximating a warm oven – it was sweltering.

The journey was usually a jolly affair. Someone always started a tune and we all joined in. All the usual stuff – *Ten Green Bottles*, *One Man Went To Mow*, etc. With the advent of Cliff came, '*We're All going on a Summer Holiday*'.

There were usually a couple of 'comfort stops' as the driver euphemistically called them. The men had always carried at least three crates of beer aboard, which required a stop or two en route. Added to this, some kid always wanted to be sick, after stuffing his face on the packed sandwiches – 'over excitement' my Mam would always exclaim. I remember one lad's mother telling us, 'He has a weak stomach.' – Dad answered, 'Weak stomach? – he seemed to be chucking it a fair distance.' Mam glared at him, but Dad was on his third Brown Ale and grinning at his own joke.

During the journey, the kids would play travel games, like trying to spot cars of a certain colour, or the first one to see the sea. One of my favourite games was 'pub cricket'. If a pub name had arms and legs in it – for instance, The Queen's Arms, that would count as two. The Horse and Jockey would be eight. If the next pub was something like The Crown, you had been bowled out. I once got The Horse and Hounds as one of my pubs. I asked my Dad how many hounds were in a hunt, and he said, 'Not a clue – about a hundred?' I declared my innings!

Shortly before the arrival, someone would walk round the coach and thrust a flat cap in our direction. It was a 'whip round' for the driver. Everyone threw a few coins in the cap. It always contained more money on the outward journey. On the return journey everyone was broke!

We would arrive at the camp site and collect our suitcases from the storage area of the coach and head towards reception. We would collect our keys and head off to find our chalet (or digs as they were often called by the older ones). We were here, and the holiday had started!

After lugging our suitcases round the camp site a couple of times, we would finally find the right chalet or caravan, Dad would open the door and we would all pile in. Mam would inspect the whole place and periodically 'tut' at something before proclaiming, 'It'll do.'

We kids were like Ninja's. We had already mentally mapped out the place from the brochure and knew where the beach, the swimming pool and the amusement arcade were positioned. The only decision to make was what order we went to visit them all in.

One fond memory I have was that you could hire a sort of four wheeled cycle with a bench seat, two sets of pedals and two sets of handlebars on it. It was great for me. My two sisters did all the pedalling while I sat between them on the bench seat. They later told me that "it felt like trying to pedal a tractor".

A lot of the time was spent on the beach with Mam and Dad sunning themselves on a couple of hired deck chairs while we played with our buckets and spades on the sand. I remember the whole sensory overload of that beach. The seagulls screaming and wheeling as they swooped down to steal a chip or two from some unsuspecting victim. The smell of the sea and the warm sand intermingled with the delicious aroma of the sugary smell from the candy floss stall and the smell of chips being cooked. Added to this was the gentle lapping of the waves and the excited screams of delight from the kids running around and playing. It was a million miles away from our little northern mill town.

I would ask Mam if I could have some money for the arcade. I knew I had some spends put aside that she kept in her handbag, but I would ask her for some money. I could spend mine later. By the third day I asked her if I could have some money for the arcade and she would say, 'Sorry, you can't' – I would protest and say, 'What about my money in your handbag?' She would then say, 'What do you think you have been spending?'

Mam would always buy me a donkey ride. The donkeys were so well trained, they would just trot the allotted distance, stop and turn around again and come back all on their own. One particular donkey on one such trip decided that it must be dinnertime. It covered the distance in double quick time at a stiff canter, turned on a sixpence almost depositing me on the sand and came cantering back again. Everyone thought it hilarious, but I had developed a temporary sense of humour bypass.

Fitted in to the week was always a visit to at least one castle and, of course, a trip to the fair. Mam was always generous at the funfair. We went on whatever rides we fancied (well, the ones we were old enough for). When I think back it would not have been possible to be any happier.

Sadly, and all too soon, our time in the sun was up and we reluctantly packed our stuff (including a few tacky 'Present From Rhyl' souvenirs and assorted pebbles and shells from the beach). We boarded the coach again. No singing on this trip!

Some kids were blubbing at having to leave their personal Shangri La's behind and they were being comforted by their mothers and bribed with sticks of rock or big, garishly coloured lollipops that were made up of three or four different coloured sections of boiled sugar, put together to resemble the face of a cat.

Soon the beauty of the Welsh Coast gave way to a more industrial landscape – back to reality!

I remember a sort of melancholy seeping through my bones, but Mam would say things like, 'I'll be glad to be sleeping in my own bed tonight,' and 'There's nothing like coming home.' I would silently disagree!

We would arrive back at our house and open the door. The house would smell familiar, but strangely unlived in! The kettle would immediately go on and Mam would borrow a drop of milk from an obliging neighbour until she could get round to the shops later. Dad would probably already be on the sofa and falling asleep.

I could go out to play with my mates to tell them about all my adventures. They would remark upon things like, 'Ee, I can see you've got a sun-tan.' Then ask if I had brought them anything back. I would lie and say that I had and we would go back to my house and

I would give them a stick of rock between them that I had bought for personal consumption.

All was back to normal. It seemed like it had all been a wonderful dream, until I reached into my pocket for my hanky to find my pockets had sand in them and a sea shell. There was only one week of the summer holidays left. It made the misery complete when I realised I had school again in a another week.

Sayings

Mam was a weaver. This meant that her hearing had been impaired by years of working in horrendous noise with no ear protection. The law firms today would be having a field day in compensation claims! A side effect of this was that Mam never said anything 'Sotto Voce'. Dad would say that she could whisper over three fields, Huddersfield, Chesterfield and Macclesfield.

She also had odd ways of wording things. This was brought hilariously to life by Peter Kay during his comedy routines. Mam would say things like, 'I will go uptown now so I can get back.' The odd part is, I never ever questioned it. I knew what she meant. I remember a school friend asking me why Mam said that, and I just looked at him in puzzlement and said, 'Well she means that if she sets off now, she can get back.' He just shook his head and pretended to understand. She would also ask me questions like, 'Do you want to feel the back of my hand?' – I knew she didn't want me to check if she had applied hand cream that morning!

Another thing she said is, 'You can tell you are your Dad's son.' whenever I did anything wrong. She once said this in front of one of my teachers, who looked at her in complete bewilderment as if there may have been some initial doubt about my parentage!

Friday was always traditionally chippy night. Me being the youngest, it was usually me who had to go. Mam would write down the order on a piece of paper and put it in a paper bag along with the money. At the chip shop, I would just hand the bag across to them.

This one particular day, she said to me, 'When you walk in, just say to them can you do me a fish without.' Now Dad was the wind-up merchant. I thought Mam had also started branching out into the family sport too. So I asked her, 'A fish without what?'. She told me not to give her any cheek and just to say it, and that they would know what I meant.

I arrived at the chippy. I cleared my throat and said, 'Mam says can you do her a fish without?' I fully expected the room to dissolve into laughter. The woman behind the counter just said, 'OK luv.' I found out later it meant that she wanted a fish cooked with just enough batter to keep it in one piece whilst they fried it.

Mam would also regularly mispronounce words. One of her favourites being to pronounce pneumonia as 'pewmonia'. Thus vests were worn until June, because, as Mam would say, 'I don't want you catching pewmonia and dying on me.'

When my eldest sister got married, Mam became quite friendly with her new son-in-law's Mum. Mam said that he calls her Mum because they come from Burnley and they are posh up there!

One day, the two mothers were chatting as they often did and she said to Mam that she suffered terribly from Cystitis. Some time later, I was on the bus with Mam as we were off to town to buy me some shoes. As happened quite often, if the bus driver was ahead of schedule he would park up en route, switch off the engine and wait a while. All would go quiet and you would hear polite chatter between the women on the bus. It was at this moment that Mam decided to also break into conversation with a neighbour sitting across from her. Mam's voice rang out loudly. People on the top deck could probably hear her. She said to our neighbour, 'Oh she does suffer badly, my son-in-law's mother. She has that...oh what's it called now....oh I remember, Syphilis'. Instantly, all the chatter from the other passengers stopped. You could have heard a pin drop. I sank down further into my seat. 'No Mam,' I said, 'it's cystitis'. Mam said,

'Well I knew it was something like that.'

I also remember once being ill and being sent in to school with a note to hand in on my return. The teachers passed the note around and all guffawed with laughter. Apparently Mam couldn't spell diarrhoea so had written, 'He's had the trots and not been off the toilet all night.'

It's a wonder I didn't grow up with a complex! Some people think that Alan Bennett's writings are in some way exaggerated or a caricature written to amuse. They don't go half the distance they could in reality! That's the way we roll Up North!

Summer 1967 – Staying Up Late

The evening was set to be a notable one. Dad had brought home some of the memorable characters from the pub and a couple of crates of beer. It was my summer holidays so no school, and all thoughts set for naught but enjoyment. I could smell the pub on them as they entered our kitchen. Soon they were all scattered about the room, each with a mug of tea and some of Mam's baking.

A little later, the glasses came out and the beer flowed. The shadows on the wall flickered with the glow from the burning coals and birch logs. Tobacco drifted by with the delicious smell of cooking and the drying herbs by the fireside, mixing together uniquely to pull me deeper into it all. I was amongst the princes of story-telling. The bards of my youth. Old men's tales flowed freely, as did the beer.

"Back when" tales and fondly remembered old names were regaled with reverence. The tales re-told with such finesse, they became almost tactile, sinuous and lithe. The story of how 'Johnny Jobby' earned his title, and the night Dad stumbled into the pigsty and ended up 'covered in it' – we all knew what 'it' was but old Billy actually said it. The liquid time rolled by, the magnificence of this lost age excited my mind and the tales so colourful fell thunder-like upon my ears, leaving my mind set for warmer joyous stories. I surrendered to the helpless and tear-falling laughter of the timeless, natural warmth that surrounded this happy band of part-time rogues and raconteurs.

A half-broken morning light and a fire that spat and died a little heralded the weary bedtime walk to bliss, and soon I was within the arms of a godlike sleep ...and my dreams? They were the borrowed dreams and coloured ribbons that fell from the hearts of those aged warriors. As Dad would say, 'There's nowt like pitmen for tellin' a good tale.'

1961 – Defending My Nanna

Nanna and Grandad's house was always a welcoming place, to which I was always a welcome visitor. They only lived four doors down from us. Consequently, I was never away from the place. Many is the time I remember us playing Dominoes on the kitchen table. Grandad (or 'Mi father' as I always called him) believed it helped to teach me to count accurately and quickly. We would also play Ludo or Snakes and Ladders. I have no idea what they taught me. I think that Grandad secretly liked playing them too! Most of the time though, I just amused myself.

Nanna had a big, old-fashioned looking tin that had once contained biscuits. It was now the repository for all her buttons. This would keep me occupied for ages. There were hundreds in there. I would ask her such questions as, 'What are these brass buttons off Nanna?' And she would weave some story about a uniform of one of my uncles she had taken them off, after something she called de-mob. I had no idea what de-mob was, but it sounded exciting and was obviously in the days of people with metal buttons.

One particular day, I happened to be playing on the floor when my cousin came in. He lived two doors down between my house and Nanna's. He was almost a year older than me. Nanna called us both over and took out a bag of sweets from her apron pocket. She told us to take one each. He tried to sneak two out of the bag. Nanna told him to put it back. He then threw a bit of a petulant fit. He called Nanna a fat pig and kicked her in her shins.

That was it – the red mist had descended. 'Don't you kick my Nanna!' I said to him before I flew at him like a boy possessed. In a second I had him on the floor and was raining down punches on him.

Grandad had witnessed the kicking event. Nanna was shouting, 'Break them up, Fred, break them up!' Grandad said, 'I will do no such thing – that lad is defending you.' After a few seconds more, Grandad lifted me away from the now sobbing cousin with the words, 'He's had enough lad, let him be now.' I had the feeling that Grandad was secretly proud of me.

On my way home, I had to walk past his house. The backyards were open so it was one, big, communal space. As I walked past his house his mother sprang out of her back door and grabbed my arm. She then pinned both of my arms behind my back and said to her son, 'Go on, lay into him.' As luck would have it, my Mam just happened to be walking out with a basket of washing to peg on the line. Mam dropped the basket and was on her like a flash.

She grabbed her hair and flung her to the ground. I had never seen Mam like this – she was like a demon. 'If you lay one finger on my son again, EVER, I will beat you to a pulp.' She then went on to inform her that she was nothing but a bully, and that she was all puff and wind. She also said that if her son couldn't fight his own battles then she had bred a little coward.

She led me away with the words, 'Come on, our David, if she touches you again, you tell me.' I was impressed by Mam. She was mostly meek and mild, but when needs be, she was made of sterner stuff!

When we arrived home Dad asked Mam what all the shouting had been about. Mam snapped back at him with, 'Nowt, it's just that woman two doors down, it's all sorted now.' Dad knew better than to press her further on the subject, so he just nodded and went back to his newspaper. When Mam asked me what had triggered the event, I told her the whole story. She just smiled at me then, strangely, told me that I shouldn't fight – a bit rich coming from her! She then gave me a huge hug that almost took the wind out of me and she said, 'That's my lad, you protect your Nanna.' She then kissed me on my forehead and gave me threepence out of her purse.

David Hayes

1960s – Getting Lines

One of the bizarre punishments I remember from school were 'Lines'. What a complete waste of time, ink and paper they were! For anyone who is unaware of this punishment, it involved writing out the same sentence over and over a set amount of times. Usually multiples of ten. The usual punishment was a hundred lines. They always started with the same three words. Either, 'I must not' or 'I will not'. You had a set amount of time to complete the task. The teacher usually asked us to hand them in the day after.

Most times these were done at the kitchen table at home. Mam would see me writing away and glance over my shoulder at what I was writing. She would instantly pass judgement. Something along the lines of, 'That'll teach you'. Sometimes this was endorsed by a smack across the back of the head. She became used to me doing lines. I remember discussing this with a friend recently. He laughed and said 'Lines? – yes I remember those! I did more lines than a track-laying company.'

I remember writing another set of lines at the kitchen table, but also trying to shield them from Mam. She insisted that I show her. I had written, ' I must not break wind loudly in class.' Her face was like thunder. 'Haven't I brought you up better than that?' she said.

I replied, 'Yes, you have, but it wasn't me.'

She asked me over and over to tell the truth. I ended up yelling at her something along the lines of, 'I'm telling you I didn't sodding do

175

it!'. She then asked me why the teacher had given me the lines. When I told her that no one would own up to it, so he gave us all lines – even the girls. Mam seemed to become angry.

She told me to stop writing the lines immediately. She then sat down, penned a note and put it into an envelope. She said that I was to give it to the teacher if he asked why I hadn't done the lines as requested.

The very next day came and the teacher asked that exact question. He said, 'Where are your lines, Hayes?

I replied, 'I haven't done them, Sir. Mam said I mustn't do them. I then handed him the envelope. Before opening it, he shouted at me, 'I'M YOUR TEACHER, NOT YOUR MOTHER, AND YOU WILL DO AS YOU ARE TOLD!'. He then opened up the envelope, read the note and broke into a spontaneous guffaw of laughter that wasn't in the least bit ironic. He told me to wait where I was. He went to another colleague in the next classroom, through an adjoining door and showed her the note. She burst out laughing too.

When he returned he was still chuckling. He said to me, 'Well, your mother has given me the best laugh in months. Sit down, boy.' He then carried on with the lessons.

I found out from a friend that my mother and her letter had become the stuff of legend around the school. One boy had sneaked the letter out of the teacher's drawer and read it. It apparently said. 'You may punish my son when he has done something wrong, but not when he hasn't. As for breaking wind, it was probably you who did it in the first place and tried to blame it on the children.' It is a kind of logic that's difficult to argue with, isn't it?

1960s Going Out Tooled Up

As kids we had an arsenal of innocuous and home-made weapons. We had throwing arrows. These were oversized arrows that were weighted at the pointed end. Just below the flights was a little groove. You had a piece of string approximately the same length as the arrow. You wrapped the string around your hand and the other end you wrapped a couple of times around the notch near the flights. This had the effect of doubling the length of your throwing arm. You held the arrow at the pointed end like a dart then threw it with an extended arm. We reached some decent distances with them.

Another piece of kit was what we called a 'Clay Clodder'. This was nothing but a length of willow of maybe four or five feet long. It had to be a wood with a whippy action. On to the end of this was squeezed a blob of clay. You whipped the piece of wood towards the intended target and the lump of clay would come flying off. It was a delicate action. Too fast and the clay would come off before being thrown. Too slow and it would either just stay on or land a few feet away. Once you found the sweet spot you could get the stuff to fly for yards and yards.

One for the classroom assassins was the rubber band catapult. You stretched a rubber band between your thumb and first finger to make the catapult. The projectiles were bits of paper that were folded over and over until they made a hard, V shaped pellet. This was then hooked on to the catapult. This usually resulted in a red mark on someone's neck.

We would usually buy our pea shooters because they were relatively cheap, but we had been known to make them out of aluminium aerial tubing from the old H or X shaped aerials. Our ammunition of choice was Black Peas (sometimes called Maple Peas or Pigeon Peas); these were readily available from the local pet shop and a 1lb bagful would last ages. The more skilled exponents of this particular weapon could shovel a small handful of these peas into their mouths and fire them off in rapid succession in machine gun fashion.

About this time, the toy makers bought out a realistic looking hand gun called The Sekiden. It came complete with fifty silver plastic balls. You could load all these into the gun and it would fire them off one by one each time you pulled the trigger. They came out at a decent velocity – far faster than a pea shooter. Obviously, the plastic balls were very soon lost, but the good old black peas made an admirable substitute. Boys would wander around the playground with these tucked into their belts, meting out summary justice to anyone they didn't like.

The weapon of mass destruction: The prince among weapons was the catapult. We would cut a Y shaped section out of a tree to make the catapult body. We called it a 'two-leg'. We would go uptown to a sports shop and buy something we called Partridge Elastic. This was black rubber solid elastic that was square in section. Usually about 3/16 of an inch thick. This would be cut into two equal lengths, laid over the end of the two leg and bound tight with string. A flat leather strip was fastened between the two lengths of elastic to make a pouch, and you were hot to trot.

These catapults were no toys. You could do some serious damage with them. The ammo of choice was ball bearings when we could get them. You could whack these out so hard that sometimes you could get them to stick into wood. Failing that, we used small stones. I

178

remember one particular episode where we found an old crab apple tree growing on some waste ground. There were hundreds of little hard apples, both on the branches and lying on the ground. We filled our pockets with as many as we could carry and went off to cause mischief.

We ended up in an old, disused colliery yard and decided that we would break up into two teams and try to ambush each other using our catapults as weapons. You soon learned to be nimble on your feet as these things bloody hurt when they hit you! I happened to be skulking behind an old, rusty water tank when I heard someone say, 'HEY HAYZEE!' I turned to look who it was and saw one of the other team some fifteen yards or so away. Just as I turned, he let fly with an apple and hit me square in the middle of my top lip. I dropped like a sack of potatoes and saw drips of blood on my shirt.

We ambled off towards home. I had stemmed the bleeding with my hankie but my lip had come up a treat. It altered my speech, it was that bad. One lad said to me, 'You look like a duck.'

As older boys, we saved up and bought a sort of air pistol called The Gat. This fired ·177 calibre air rifle pellets. These were awful. They consisted of a tube within the barrel that had a spring inside it. The tube stuck out of the front by around four inches. When you pushed the tube in, this tensioned the spring and pushed the tube so it was now level with the back of the gun. You then unscrewed a little needle shaped thing from the back. You put a pellet into the vacant hole and pushed it home with the needle shaped thing which was then screwed back into place.

To say they were inaccurate was a gross understatement. You could stand ten feet away from the intended target (usually a can or a bottle) and you would be lucky if you hit anything. You could miss by as much as a foot! Even when you hit the bottle it would just make a 'TINK' noise and it would fall over. We would push the tube back in with our hands, but this was painful and left a series of little, ring-shaped welts on our hands. We usually ended up by either pushing it in against a tree or a wall.

I think I was around sixteen before I bought a proper, break-barrel air rifle. It was a Diana ·22. Even then I only bought it because I could! It was at that time when girls were proving to be more of an interest. I suppose it truly was 'make love not war'.

~~~~~~~~~~~~~~~~~~

David Hayes

What Has He Done Now?

Lightning Source UK Ltd.
Milton Keynes UK
UKHW03f0515040418
320495UK00001B/12/P